SUPERBOB!

The Bob Taylor Story

To Mark
Happy Birthday
Best Wishes
Bob Taylor

Glenn Willmore & John Homer

**Perspective
Publishing**

Also available from PERSPECTIVE PUBLISHING

Bomber Brown: The Tony Brown Story	ISBN 0 9534626 0 9
Albion Review 1999	ISBN 0 9534626 1 7
Albion Review 2000	ISBN 0 9534626 2 5
Albion Review 2001	ISBN 0 9534626 3 3
Albion Review 2002	ISBN 0 9534626 4 1
Albion Review 2003	ISBN 0 9534626 7 6
King of The Hawthorns: The Jeff Astle Story	ISBN 0 9534626 5 X
SuperBob! The Bob Taylor Story	ISBN 0 9534626 6 8

First published in Great Britain in 2003 by
PERSPECTIVE PUBLISHING
54 Newhall Street
West Bromwich
West Midlands B70 7DJ8

ISBN 0 9534626 6 8

Concept, book and cover design by Glenn Willmore

Printed and bound in Great Britain by The Bath Press, Bath

FOREWORD

Once every generation or so, a footballer arrives at the Albion who the fans instantly take into their hearts. It is difficult to define what makes that sort of player. Goals help — the more the better — but character, determination, and an empathy with the club and its supporters are just as important.

Jeff Astle was that player in the Sixties. Bob Taylor was that player in the Nineties. His goals brought light in the darkness that were the 'Wilderness Years' at West Bromwich Albion. He brought promotion to the club in 1993 when it had sunk to its lowest level, he helped keep them up again almost every year after that and, when he returned from Bolton in 2000, kept them up again. He got them to the Play-offs in 2001 and won them promotion to the Premiership in 2002. This book, written to commemorate Bob's Testimonial Season, in 2003, tells Bob's story, from Horden Colliery Welfare, to the Premiership. I hope you all — Bristol City, Leeds, Bolton and Albion fans alike — enjoy reading it.

If anyone has any doubts about what high regard Bob is held in West Bromwich, then they should read what follows. It's a Bob Taylor joke, passed around in late March 2003, on an Albion fans' internet chatroom. And remember, Bob has only started one game this season, and has not scored a goal in almost a year...

Bob Taylor, Michael Owen and David Beckham are standing before God at the throne of Heaven. God looks at them and says, "Before granting you a place at my side, I must first ask you what you believe in." Addressing David Beckham first, he asks, "What do you believe?" David looks God in the eye and states passionately, "I believe football to be the food of life. Nothing else brings such unbridled joy to so many people, from the slums of Rio to the bright lights of Barcelona. I have devoted my life to bring such joy to people who stood on the terraces supporting their club." God looks up and offers David the seat to his left. He then turns to Michael Owen. "And you, Mike, what do you believe?" Michael stands tall and proud. "I believe courage, honour and passion are the fundamentals of life, and I've spent my whole playing career providing a living embodiment of these traits." God, moved by the passion of the speech, offers Michael the seat to his right. Finally, he turns to Bob Taylor. "And you, Mr Taylor, what do you believe?" "I believe," says Bob, "that you're sitting in my seat."

Glenn Willmore
March 2003

Unless football changes dramatically. Bob Taylor might well be the last Albion player to have a Testimonial Year. The game is not the same now as it was when Bob started his professional career at Leeds United.

Bob has seen the introduction of all-seater stadia and the Premier League, and he was helped Albion rise from the Third Division into the Premiership itself. Throughout it all, two words epitomise Bob Taylor. Goals – and honesty.

He has always scored goals – some pretty vital ones at that, but above all, he has always struck me as an honest player. Never one to shirk a challenge or a tackle, always ready to be frank about his own performance – and always ready to take time out for the fans.

When we first put the concept of this book to him, Bob was gob-smacked. His honest opinion was, "There'll be nothing to write about." How wrong you were – Super Bobby Taylor.

John Joseph Homer

This book is dedicated to my family and friends – and the supporters of West Bromwich Albion. My story is not just about me, it's just as much about the fans. They've lifted me up and kept me going. I know how fickle some fans can be, but even when I wasn't here they still sang my name and supported me. Thanks a million.

Bob Taylor

Acknowledgments
We would like to thank the following for their vital contributions to this book: Donald Taylor, Kath and Trevor Parkinson, Bobby Gould, Kevin Grice (for all the wonderful Albion goal photographs), Dave Hewitt (for all the other great Albion pictures), Dave Holloway, Sean Gascoigne, Michael Stanley, Amanda Hume, for a super proof-reading job and, last, but not least, Bob Taylor himself, for some great memories.

On the furniture wagon

Bob Taylor was born in the north-east – always a hotbed for the production of young footballers, desperate to get out of the pits, on February 3 1967. "I was born in Littlethorpe Hospital, and Littlethorpe is classed as Easington, County Durham, because it's just over the border. Sometimes I say I was born in Horden, which is just a stone's throw away. But really, I suppose, you have to say I was born in Easington, but brought up in Horden, of course, and lived there all my life."

As with so many youngsters, Bob started to get interested in football at school, as a seven or eight year-old, kicking the ball about in the playground every day with his schoolfriends. Being the north-east, he did have other players to follow and look up to. "I think one of the lads who stood out in the village, in football terms, was Brian Honour, who later played for over ten years at Hartlepool. I won't say I idolized him, but he was the best player that I'd ever seen, and I knew I wanted to be like him. I ended up playing in the same school side as Brian had, and I sort of took over as the team captain in that side when he left."

There was no football connection in the family. "My Dad never played – he wasn't athletic, but my Mum did a bit of running at one time, long distance running for the County, but that's all. I don't know where my football side comes from."

Bob — wearing number five — displaying his school team's haul of trophies

Bob's sister Glenda was always interested in football, as Bob's father, Don, explains. "She's a real all-rounder. She played for Sunderland Ladies football team, and she's good at golf, hockey, cricket and tennis. When she use dto come to matches with me, to watch Bob for Peterlee and Horden, she used to play 'keepy-uppy' with the ball — and the crowd used to stop watching the game and watch her instead!"

Horden was a classic village community. When Bob was a youngster, virtually everybody in the village either worked down the pit, or had several members of the family who did. Things have changed dramatically since then. "There's not a lot left in Horden nowadays; it's like a ghost town, because the main source of income was the pit, and now, of course, the pit is closed. Everybody in the village worked at the pit, and it was a very close community. My Dad worked in the pit, and my Grandad, and my Dad's two brothers – in a way, it was passed down across the generations, and when I left school, I had my name put down at the pit as well, but obviously, by then, there weren't the opportunities, and I had to wait my time after leaving school, being on the dole, doing YTS schemes, and so on. In other words, in between playing games at the weekends, and snooker at night – just being a lay-about around the house!"

Bob has fond memories of his father's fishing trips with his mates from the mine. "I used to go with them, and on Saturday nights they all used to come back to Mum's house, and she'd put a big pan of broth on – broth and dumplings – and I grew up with that; with the Seventies

Left, Bob proudly holds onto the cup. Player number three is Ian Frith, still wearing his wrist cast, courtesy of Bob. Right, Bob shows off the cup to the rest of the school

records playing in the background, as I remember. It was open house, really."

Bob might not have had the family connections with the 'beautiful game,' but he soon developed a love for the professional sport. "I used to watch *Match of The Day* – with my Dad – and as now, when all the kids support Manchester United, I used to support Liverpool. I was an armchair fan; I had the pictures and posters up on the wall of all the players. At that time it was the era of Keegan and Toshack, and I enjoyed the scoring side of it, even though, at that time, I wasn't a striker, I was a defender. I was particularly impressed with Kevin Keegan, because he used to score a lot of goals for such a small lad."

Bob may have classed himself as a Liverpool supporter, but he actually saw very little professional football 'in the flesh' – because he was too busy playing himself. He would train on Thursday, then play on Saturday and Sunday, every week. On the odd occasion when he did manage to get to a game, he would go with his mates to watch Sunderland or Newcastle.

Strangely, as a youngster, Bob was always a defender, at least in his early days. He played for his junior school as a full-back, but as he got older his headmaster, Peter Dunn – who ran the school side – put him at centre-half, where he remained right up to senior school, apart from when he captained the County side, when he reverted to full-back. He was instructed by Mr Dunn never to leave his own half, so he only ever scored two goals for the juniors — and one of those was a shot from his own half, some feat for a ten year old! "We were a good team, winning cups every year. My Dad used to drum it into me, to keep playing, to progress in the game, but nobody ever came in for me as a youngster." Yet to start with, Don was not even aware that his son was in the school side. "He didn't tell us! I was out on the beach fishing when a close friend of mine, Albert Hogg, came up, and told me that he had seen our Robert playing for the school. He said he was fantastic, and I couldn't believe it, so I made sure I was there the next time. And he was brilliant. All these young bairns were chasing the ball, but Robert stood and waited for the pass. I was amazed that he was a class above the rest; and he hardly missed a game after that."

Don remembers the day Bob broke the wrist of one of his team mates. "Ian Frith was his name. I asked him if he done it deliberately, and he said 'Of course not. I was taking shots at him in goal, and he saved one — but it broke his wrist!'"

It was not until senior school that Bob switched to a forward role, and then only by accident. "We were getting hammered, week in, week out, and the teacher decided to swap us round, me and the centre-forward, so I went up front and the centre-forward went centre back. And it worked really well; we didn't lose many games then, and I started scoring goals, and never looked back."

Bob was now fifteen, an age when, even then, scouts were usually starting to show an interest. There were other lads in the County side who had trials with League clubs; Alan Plant with Ipswich, Tommy Garside, with Sunderland, and Robbie Turner, who was at Wimbledon with the Crazy Gang, and who would later play up front with Bob at Bristol City. "I had a trial at Newcastle, which my Dad fixed up because he knew a scout at St James' – but that was just a case of turning up on the night and playing a game. It was a case of twenty of their apprentices trying to get to know one person's name – mine – and I was there in the dressing room trying to get their names, and remember them when I got out on the pitch. It didn't really work out — 'Thanks, but no thanks.'" Don was always pushing young Robert. "I knew he would make it. He was always determined to play the game. I remember Liverpool were looking at him, and they wrote to us, but nothing came of it. But he was determined."

Bob was more successful with a second trial, again fixed up by a 'friend of a friend' of his father, at Hartlepool. "I ended up training with them on a Thursday, and playing for one of their sides on a Saturday, in the Northern Intermediate League. Now, of all the teams I was playing for then, I was 'scoring goals for fun,' you know – but I think I only scored one for Hartlepool, at that time. I was uncomfortable then, and I told my Dad that I wanted to pack it all in." Don's reaction was

Bob (fourth from left, front row) with his Sunday team, Horden Comrades

unequivocal – he threatened to burn Bob's boots, and stop him playing at all! In the end, though, Bob had his way, and turned his back on the League club, opting to play for his local non-League side, Horden Colliery Welfare.

By now, Bob was sixteen, and had left school. "I wasn't too good, as regards the academic side. I was too interested in playing football. Looking back now, I sometimes wish I'd put more into that side of things, but it was always football for me. I was told to pick three choices before going into the careers room, and I picked 'footballer, footballer, footballer.' And I was told – 'Come on, kid, what are you going to be? Think about it. Pick a lorry-driver, or a docker.' Obviously, my choices were as a footballer – or down the pit, I suppose."

But by then, even the pit had gone, closing for the last time in 1986, so Bob went on a year long YTS scheme run by Age Concern. "The girls went to the care homes, and the lads did courses in brick-laying and joinery, and painting and decorating. We went out to old people in the area, and painted their bathrooms, or built them a wall – sometimes even when they wanted us to! We'd do the work for nothing, and they'd just have to pay for the cost of materials. We'd just be 'helping the community.'"

At the end of the YTS, Bob signed on the dole – "Just playing my snooker and picking up my giro; and, obviously, playing my football." A mis-spent youth – for a while – meant that Bob's snooker was improving fast — his best break was now 54, but it enraged his mother. "He's always down the Welfare, playing snooker. Get his name down

Horden Colliery FC — a far cry from The Hawthorns and Wembley...

9

for that colliery!" Then Bob got a break of a different sort. "My Sunday League manager, Frankie Dean, who was the bin driver with the local council, somehow wangled it to get me a job with the council. I started off first on the furniture wagon. It was a big, metal-framed wagon, and people rang up if they wanted fridges or three piece suites taking away and me and this guy would go round and put them in the wagon, and take them down to the tip."

After that, it was the bin wagon proper – "I was on that for about thirteen weeks. They were the very heavy metal bins – the ones with hot ashes – not the plastic ones you get nowadays; they had fires in them, and everything. The pay was good, and even though you started at six or seven o'clock in the morning, you were finished by two o'clock in the afternoon, if you got your round done. And then it was back to the snooker hall!" Ironically, in later years, one of Bob's nicknames at the Albion would be 'Trigger' because of his resemblance to the binman from Only Fools and Horses.

Bob's Sunday League side was Horden Comrades Welfare FC, whilst on Saturdays he was playing for the Peterlee junior side, for whom, in his second season, he scored sixty goals as the side won a League and Cup Double. When he was seventeen, he started playing for Horden Colliery Welfare in the Dryborough League. "Everybody thought I'd naturally sign for the Peterlee first team, but I was a Horden lad – and I was playing for Horden cricket team in the summer – so I signed for them instead. The two grounds, football and cricket, are side by side, and the guy who ran part of the cricket club, 'Spot' Matthews, was also with the football club, and he invited me to train with the footballers."

Bob's (far right, front row) Saturday side, Peterlee Juniors, complete with the Horner Cup

The Dryborough Northern League was a tough one to play in for a seventeen year old, but Bob reckoned he had had a good grounding in the Sunday League. " You got used to the physical side of it – guys coming out of the pub at twelve o'clock for a two o'clock kick-off, all pissed up, you know. You got used to it, and you learn the hard way, and grow up that way.

Bob would do anything for a game, as Don recalled. "One Sunday morning Robert was in bed when the manager of Horden Comrades knocked on the door to ask if he would play — for the over-forties side! I said no, but Bob was down in a flash to play. When he came back, his ankle was in a real state. He's trod in a hole and turned his ankle. For a day or two his Mam treated it with bandages soaked in vinegar, but he could hardly walk, and he had to use a broom as a crutch. In the end, I told him to go to the beach and walk a mile up the coast, and back again. He didn't believe it would work, but I told him it worked for horses —and it would for him. And the next day he was right as rain. But his ankle was always a problem until he joined Leeds, who sorted it out for him."

At that time, Horden Colliery were going through a hard time themselves, and were a shadow of the side Bob remembered sneaking in to watch for free as a kid. "They had big crowds in those days, and were a really good side, flying high at the top of their division. But by the time I started playing, the crowds had really gone down, and I was playing for ten quid a game, and we were just getting the real ardent supporters, week in, week out."

It was then that Bob got his second big break, when Horden appointed the former Sunderland full-back Dick Malone as their new manager. "Dick Malone was something of a pull, a new name, a new face. When he first came, I didn't really know who he was. I remember, when Sunderland won the Cup in 1973, my Mum ordered a big colour poster from the *Sun*, and it had all the players' faces on it, and the Montgomery save against Leeds. When Dick came, I went back and had a look at that, and there he was. But then he had this big bouffant hairstyle, you know, and curly hair. He'd come, and he was bald on top, and he was a tall, skinny bloke, compared to the pictures."

But Dick Malone was to play an important part in setting Bob off onto the career of a professional footballer. "I hadn't had time to get to know Dick very well before I left. Sometimes we'd turn up for training, and Dick wouldn't be there, because of his work commitments. His assistant, Geoff Cranson, would take us for training then. He was the brother of Ian Cranson, from Stoke City. But Dick was always there on a Saturday, of course."

After three months at the club, in December 1985, Malone recommended Bob – his team's top scorer – to Leeds United, ironically the side that Malone's Sunderland had so embarrassed in the 1973 FA Cup Final. Leeds' chief scout at that time was Dave Blakey, and he invited the youngster over to Elland Road for a month's trial. It came as quite a shock to Bob. "I turned up for training one Tuesday night, and Dick told me not to bother changing, because I had to go home and pack. I was going to Leeds. 'Oh no I'm not!' 'Oh yes you are!' It was the pantomime season, after all. I was adamant that I wasn't going. And Dick was just as certain. 'Yes you are; you're Mum's packing your things, and you're going tomorrow!'"

For the seventeen year old, it was a real trip into the unknown. "I was off to Leeds, but at that time, I'd hardly ever been out of Horden. I think the farthest I'd ever been was to Skegness, to the holiday camp, on the coach with my Mum and Dad. It was a big, big move for me, and I was scared, and I didn't want to go. I thought it was going to be like the Newcastle trial, and I wondered if I might be out of my depth – I was really scared."

This was no rushed affair, like at Newcastle. Leeds took Bob on trial for a month, and treated him like one of the apprentices. "They trained me and worked on me, with weights and everything. And I mucked in. Although I was nearly eighteen, I did the jobs of an apprentice, at sixteen. Cleaning boots, picking up the laundry, washing cars, looking after the staff, making cups of tea – all the sorts of things that apprentices did in those days. It was a change from carting bins around – but you got to play football as well. You see, I didn't just go in as a pro' – I had to do the menial jobs as well, and learn that way."

Bob in the strip of mighty Leeds United

Under the watchful eye of Dave Blakey, and Peter Gormby, two ex-Chesterfield pros, Bob gradually got used to the Youth team set-up at Leeds. But he was not averse to mixing with the first teamers. "Peter Gumby used to look after us, and take us for training, but we used to mix in with the first team. We'd train in the morning, come in and do our little jobs, and then maybe do weight training in the afternoons. Then Billy would get all the apprentices out and we'd have little five-a-sides between us, and it was great. Billy was a great manager to play for."

Bob got off to a great start to his Leeds career. He made his debut in the third team, playing against York City in the Northern Intermediate League that he had signally failed to impress in with Hartlepool. This time, Bob was fitter, older — slightly — and definitely more worldly-wise. Playing in the York side was another great future goalscorer, Marco Gabbiadini; he scored four, but Bob finished on the winning side, with a hat-trick in a thrilling 5-4 win.

Bob's parents were all in the dark at this point. "They didn't have a phone at home in those days, so they gave me the phone number of Horden Comrades Social Club, and said 'Wednesday nights, without fail!' They went down to the Club, every Wednesday night, and waited for me to phone. And I never did – for a whole month! They never had any idea what was happening to me. In the end, they had to phone the club to find out where I was! I was in digs, in Hunslett, close to the ground. I would be working all day, walk back to my digs, then get in late at night, have my tea, and go into my bedroom – and stay there. I didn't venture out at night, I didn't know where I was. My Mam thought I'd fallen off the train! My Dad must have spoken to Dave Blakey, who told him that I'd been offered a contract – and then I got a bollocking from Dave for not phoning home as well…"

Bob scored twelve goals for the third team in the last fifteen games of that season, and signed a two year contract once he reached his eighteenth birthday. He had reached the first rung of the ladder of footballing success.

At that time, Leeds were at a low ebb. They had been relegated in 1982 – ironically, after being beaten 2-0 by Albion at The Hawthorns in their final game of the season – and the glory days of the Revie era seemed long gone. "For me it was still a massive club. You would walk around the club and there were photographs from the Don Revie era, and being there with Billy Bremner, you would get a feel for the place. After training in the afternoons, we would have a big bath together in the dressing room, and Billy would tell us all about his days with Don Revie, and playing for Scotland. There was that infamous picture with him and Keegan with their shirts off at Wembley, and Dave Mackay holding Billy by the scruff of the neck.

Bob makes the Leeds newspapers before his first team debut against Millwall — but it's Kath's Doberman, back in Barwick-in-Elmet, who gets to share top billing!

Billy was still a fiery person then. A brilliant footballer, a players' manager, and it was a privilege to be there with him. Billy brought Norman 'Bite your legs' Hunter in later, just before I left, as a coach. A big, big club, but maybe they were living in the past a little too much at that time. But you can't take it away from them – they had a great history."

By the start of the 1985-86 season, Bob had progressed into the Reserve side at Leeds. "I got to play against some of the top players in the country in the top division of the Central League. We played Liverpool – my team as a lad, of course — once and I was playing against Jan Molby, Bruce Grobbelaar –and I scored past him, in a 1-0 win at Elland Road. That was a great feeling, scoring past Grobbelaar!"

At Christmas 1985, the club released all of its young players for an extended holiday with their families, which was when Bob first met his future wife, Lesley, who lived just round the corner from the family home in Horden. When he returned to Leeds in the new year, it was to new accommodation.

"When I went back, I moved to Barwick-in-Elmet, which was about twenty miles outside Leeds, near the A1. It was a lovely village, and I stayed there for the next two and a half years. There were several other lads out there; there was me, Terry Phelan, Vinny Brockey and Lyndon Symons. I stopped with Kath and Trevor Parkinson, right next to the pub, in a quaint old village. There was a maypole in the centre of the village, and they had a traditional maypole day every three years. It was a great little community – just like being back home in Horden – and miles better than Hunslett! Kath could tell you some stories about that period... She certainly could. "When all the boys had bought their red noses, for Red Nose Day, Bob forgot and he panicked. Being Bob he got a red felt tip pen and painted his nose. Unfortunately, at the end of the day he still had a red nose, and no amount of scrubbing would remove it, so for two days he had to walk around with a sore but still very red nose. It was a real scream!" Then there was 'The Neil Diamond Incident.' "Two days before a game, Bob had a habit of buying a pound of prawns and a bottle of frascati, and going into his room to watch a video of the *Jazz Singer*, his favourite film. Once, Bob had been annoying the rest of the lads in the house, so they decided to get even. They doctored his video. Bob went to his room, which he didn't let anybody else into, sat down with his prawns and his wine and switched on the video. All we could hear through the door were death threats and abuse; the lads had replaced every song on the video with TV adverts. Bob didn't speak to anybody for two days!"

Bob Taylor made his Football League debut in a Second Division game against Millwall at Elland Road on Saturday April 12 1986. "Billy pulled me over and told me that he was putting me in the side, against Millwall. The press came over to my digs beforehand to take pictures of me, the new player, you know. Well, me and Kath's Doberman, to be exact!" Unusually for Bob, as his later career would develop, he wore the number 11 shirt — former Manchester United centre-forward Andy Ritchie was wearing number nine. Bob did not find the net, but his mate Peter Swan, a natural centre-half being played as a striker, did, in a 3-1 win. Bob kept his place the following week, but was replaced by Scott Sellars in the second half of the game, as Leeds crashed 3-0 to Crystal Palace at Selhurst Park.

It was back to the Reserves then for Bob, for the rest of the season, and he was not given another chance until the September of the 1986-87 season, in the first leg of the Littlewoods Cup against Oldham on the Astroturf at Boundary Park. Wearing the number seven shirt, Bob enjoyed the outing, recording his first senior goal with a memorable far post header, as Leeds raced into a two goal interval lead. Things were much less comfortable in the second half; Oldham fought back and Bob was withdrawn as Leeds fought a rearguard action that ended with the home side scoring three goals to win the first leg. Bob only came on as a substitute in the second leg, which Oldham won 1-0 to go through.

Bob in his first full season at Elland Road

Leeds had got off to a slow start to the season, but had gradually inched up the table, and were in sixth place by the time they took on Oldham, once again, at Elland Road on November 15. Bob played, but a 2-0 home defeat was followed by another against Birmingham City, at St Andrews, and he was out of the side again for the rest of the normal League season. As Bob watched from the sidelines, Leeds went from strength to strength, reaching the FA Cup semi-final, losing to eventual winners Coventry City. "I can remember my first visit to The Hawthorns with Leeds. It was freezing cold, with snow on the pitch, but I wasn't in the team. It was when Leeds played Telford in the FA Cup, and won 2-0." Bob was also on the sidelines at Hillsborough, four rounds later, when Leeds went out of the Cup in the semi-final.

However, that was not the end of their season, for they had finished fourth in the Second Division, and had earned a Play-off place. Leeds accounted for Oldham – for once — in the semi-finals, and were due to meet Charlton – struggling in the First Division – in the two-legged Final, which was the format employed in those early days of the Play-offs. Suddenly, Bob was a wanted man. "At the end of that season, as I was a Reserve player, they told us we could all go home. Obviously, the club was still in the Play-offs, against Charlton, but the rest of us were on holiday, so I went back home. I was with Lesley out at Finghall Abbey, near Chester-le-Street. There were no mobile phones in those days, of course, so when we got back from the Saturday afternoon out, there was a message at Lesley's parents' house – "Leeds want you back, next train!" I think they even put an SOS out for me in the newspaper, as well! So I went back, quick."

Striker John Pearson had broken his ribs in the first leg against Charlton at Selhurst Park and couldn't play in the home leg at Elland Road. "So I was in, and I remember knocking the ball past the goalkeeper, and it was in – well, on the line, with nobody in sight – and then in came Brendan Ormsby, and just banged it over the line. I said 'It's my goal' but he said, 'No – watch the replays!' And they gave it to him. But it didn't matter; it won us the game."

By the rules at that time, the win forced a replay at neutral St Andrews. Sadly, Bob did not feature in a storming match, won, after extra time, by Charlton. "I thought I might play that night, but they gave John Pearson an injection in his ribs to dull the pain, and he went out and played. I didn't even get on the substitutes' bench. They took him off, in the end, because he was struggling. I was sitting in the stands, and that was a real setback, a real sort of knock-back that you can get at times. But I'd played and done my bit in it. And at that age you're not going to throw a tantrum, although some young players might do nowadays."

The season may have ended in disappointment, but Bob had finished as the Reserves' top scorer, with 26 goals, and he was looking forward to winning a place in the first team during 1987-88.

Come the start of the new campaign, Bremner obviously thought that Bob had earned a run in the side, and he lined up in the number ten shirt, alongside John Pearson, in the opening game of the season, against Barnsley at Oakwell, and Bob got off to a great start. "I remember the goal well; the cross came over, I chested it down, and just hit it into the bottom corner." The goal that United let in that day, scored by Roger Wylde, was the only one that their defence conceded in the first five games, as they rose to fourth place in the Second Division, and it looked as if they were in for a repeat of their Play-off success of the previous season.

One of those games saw Bob play against an Albion side for the first time, in the August Bank Holiday Monday game at Elland Road. Albion had got off to a dreadful start, and relations between the board and the manager, Ron Saunders, had become very strained, to such an extent that the directors made Saunders drive to the match by car, rather than go on the team coach. John Sheridan scored an 88th minute, long range winner, and Saunders' fate was sealed. He was sacked, and Ron Atkinson took over again at The Hawthorns.

For Leeds, goals were proving hard to come by, and the team slumped, dropping as low as sixteenth by mid-October, when they crashed 6-3 to Plymouth at Home Park. But by then, Bob had hit a rich scoring vein, his seven goals in the space of ten games before the turn of the year earning him a guaranteed place in the team. Gradually, the team improved, and by the time they played their return game against the Albion at The Hawthorns, Leeds were once again challenging for the Play-offs. Bob did not make the starting line-up this time round; he had been withdrawn near the end of the previous week's home defeat by Barnsley, so he started on the bench, coming on for Rennie in the 63rd minute. By then, Leeds were 3-0 up, went on to miss a penalty, and still won 4-1, as they recorded their best-ever win at The Hawthorns.

After that, Bob was in and out of the side, scoring one more goal, at Aston Villa, as Leeds finished seventh, eight points shy of the Play-offs. "I remember my last goal for Leeds, in a 2-1 win at Villa Park. Me and Swanny scored the goals, but what I remember is that I had to play a wing-back sort of role, and Tony Daley was up against me. They kept saying to me I could mark him – Billy was saying 'You've got a good engine, you can get up and down – but it was quite something, against somebody like Daley. But I scored with a header, and Swanny got a header as well, so it was a good day, you know."

It had been a good season for Bob, one in which he had firmly established himself as a professional. In fact, excluding penalties, he had finished as his club's top scorer, with 12 goals in League and Cup, two behind John Sheridan, whose total included seven penalties. But if Bob thought that guaranteed a place in the side the following season, he was mistaken, for his career went spectacularly off track. Leeds got off to a dreadful start, recording just one win in their first dozen games, a run which saw them slump to the bottom, and Billy Bremner – whose statue now adorns the approaches of Elland Road – was sacked. In his place, they appointed Howard Wilkinson – and Bob never started another game for Leeds.

"Billy Bremner left. That's the way it goes; you just have to get on with it. Howard Wilkinson came in, and Mick Hannigan. Then the rumours went round, that Wilkinson was a hard taskmaster, but John Pearson, who was at Sheffield Wednesday with him, said he'd calmed down a lot. We did do a lot of running with him, a lot of fitness work. And a new manager wants to clear the decks, get rid of some people, bring some of his own men in. I was one of the lads he obviously didn't fancy."

Bob still has the happiest of memories about his three years at Elland Road. "Andy Ritchie was a good player, and a lovely guy, who had time for the likes of me. He's played for Manchester United, but I enjoyed playing alongside him, and he always gave words of encouragement. But the team was going through a bad time, so there was always a lot of chopping and changing, players and positions. Mervyn Day, 'Dicko' Dickinson (who went to the Albion), Ian Snodin, John Sheridan, Andy Linighan, 'Rocket' Ronnie Robinson, who also later joined the Albion, Dennis Irwin, Scott Sellars; all good players. Leeds fans were desperate for success – they were nutters, you know. The club wasn't doing so well, and the fans had a reputation at that time – but they always gave me a fair crack of the whip."

Most of all, Bob reserves the greatest respect for his manager, Billy Bremner. "Billy took David Batty under his wing – and Gary Speed as well, to a certain extent – but mainly David Batty, and if you see how he plays today, that was how Billy played. David idolized Billy, that's how much of an influence he was on him. Billy had his favourites, and obviously David Batty was one of them, but he liked players who got stuck in like that. I'm not saying I was the best player on the ball, but I got stuck in, and I wasn't afraid to get my head stuck in amongst the boots, and whether that got me a contract with Billy, I don't know. Billy had time for you, and looked after you. He had confidence in me, and, of course, he gave me my League debut."

Wilkinson re-organised the team, and after that Bob was a permanent fixture in the Reserves, appearing at The Hawthorns for the Central League game on March 8 1989, alongside other first team regulars such as John Stiles, John Pearson, Brendan Ormsby and Gary Speed. Leeds won 3-1, to help condemn Albion's second string to the Second Division. Fifteen days later, Bob was on his way out of Elland Road.

Wilkinson wanted to bring in his own men, and was casting envious glances towards Bristol City's Carl Shutt. "It just happened one day. I saw Carl Shutt at the training ground, and Wilkinson told me that Joe Jordan, the Bristol City manager, was interested in signing me. I had to go into the physio's room to talk to him. I think he was going to sign Carl Shutt anyway, so after an hour or so with Joe, I was back at my digs, getting my stuff together, and driving down to Bristol with him. I hadn't a clue where I was going. I just said 'yes' for the hell of it! I didn't really know where Bristol was – I'd certainly never been there. I didn't realise it was bloody five or six hours from the north-east!"

The deal was a cash-plus-player, with City getting Bob plus £125,000. Bob was happy financially, as well. "In the end I think I made about ten grand out of it in my hand. That was enough, because Lesley and I were saving to get married, and that meant we could go ahead. I'd signed a two year contract at Leeds, and signed a three year contract at Bristol. At Leeds, my first year I was on £120 a week, and that went up to £300 a week in the second year. I was on a similar

Bob gets off the mark at City, with his first goal against Bury

amount at Bristol, but I was getting first team football. Of course, in those days you got money in hand, to put into your bank account, or you got it back in other ways…"

Bob certainly had a 'hands-on' start to his stay at Bristol City – his new digs were in the club houses overlooking the Ashton Gate pitch! And Jordan – who was clearly a better judge of centre-forwards than Howard Wilkinson — threw him into the deep end. City had been challenging strongly for a Play-off place, until they had been side-tracked by a Littlewoods Cup run that had seen them reach the semi-final, where they had narrowly gone out to Nottingham Forest. Jordan could see that his forward line badly needed strengthening – at one stage he had defender Paul Mardon, at times wearing the eight and nine shirts – and he invested some of the money from the cup run on Taylor.

Bob well remembers his initiation into the drinking club that was Bristol City. "I arrived at Bristol, with Joe, on the Tuesday, and the club put me in a hotel. I went in to sign my contract on the Wednesday, and met the lads, and the captain, Rob Newman was there with his car, with Glenn Humphreys (who would be my best mate at City) and Russell Bromwich. They dropped me off at my digs, and then invited me to come and meet the lads. We went into town, on the main drag from Clifton, and went down this alleyway to the Revue Bar. I went in there, it was dark, and we went upstairs, and the first thing I could see in the gloom, was John Bailey (ex-Everton and Newcastle), pissed out of his head, leaning back on a stool, waving at me. And that was the first time that I met my City team mates. He managed to splutter, 'All right, how are you?' — completely drunk! He was a really funny guy – he used to do a great impression of Emlyn Hughes, when he was sober! It was a bit of a dodgy place, this Revue Bar – but we went up a few more steps at the back, and the whole team was in there, all the pros, all the reserves. Scott McGarvey, Andy Llewellyn, Mark Gavin – all big gamblers, and we just watched them playing cards and drinking in there for hours. It had been light when we went in, but it was pitch black when we left. That was my City baptism."

Bob played his first game in the red of City two days later, on Saturday March 25. His debut was in the heat of a Bristol Derby, at Rovers' cramped rented ground at Twerton Park, where a full house (of just 8,676) saw a 1-1 draw. Bob didn't score – he never did against Rovers – but he was soon off the mark the following week, against Bury. Three weeks after that, he firmly entered the hearts of City fans, when he scored his first hat-trick in a 6-1 slaughter of Huddersfield Town – "We were 5-0 up at half time, and I'd got my hat-trick by then" — and by the end of the season, he was pleased with his tally of eight goals in just twelve games. At last Bob Taylor was going places…

"Joe Jordan was great; when he had his teeth in! When he took them out – Jesus! I always visualized him as a big stocky striker in his Leeds days, but when I saw him at Bristol he was pencil-thin, tanned from his days in Italy, but toned, and muscular with great definition, but thin with it. And he could run all day, when he took us training. He was still playing when I was there – I remember him coming on once as sub for me, and scoring. But when he had his teeth out, he looked ferocious. I can remember we were training one day in Ashton Gate Park, and this guy, with a cowboy hat and a big stocky horse, just rode right through two dozen of us, with Joe in front. We all had to part, as the horse went through. Joe went crazy; just lost it. His teeth were out, he was snarling and it was "What the ****! What's going on?" in that Scottish growl of his, and he was running after the cowboy on this big horse, chasing him through the park!"

With Joe Jordan in charge at City, and Bob scoring the goals, the 1989-90 season went down in football history as a epic one for the city of Bristol. For almost all of the season its two clubs, City and Rovers, were nip and tuck at the top of the Third Division. In the early part of the season, it was Gerry Francis' Rovers who held sway. Strangely enough, they also had a former Leeds United junior as their top scorer, David Mehew heading their scoring list with 19 goals; but that was easily surpassed by Taylor. In all, Bob scored a remarkable 34 goals, in just 47 games, 27 of those coming in the League. It took City a while to get up a head of steam, but Bob was scoring from the off, netting in the opening two games against Bury and Birmingham City. It was Bob's

The second of three, in Bob's first ever League hat-trick, against Huddersfield

opening goal in the 2-0 win at Walsall on November 4 that helped send City to the top of the Third Division for the first time, a position that they kept almost to the end a gripping season.

Bob really hit form after Christmas, scoring no less than three hat-tricks – against Chester City, Swansea City and Crewe – in the space of five weeks. "Joe was a good striker, and put some good advice my way, but I was doing all right, and he didn't need to have to do much with me. You knew not to cross that line with Joe, and he got us to perform, and he did a great job at City."

City also did well in the FA Cup, and Bob scored another five goals in a run that saw City progress to the last sixteen, before being eliminated, in a second replay, by Fourth Division Cambridge. "I remember the Cup game against Chelsea, when I nearly decapitated Dave Beasant. Andy Llewellyn had had a shot, Beasant spilled it, and I came in full whack, to welly it into the net. But I completely missed the ball, as Beasant dived for it, and had I connected with his head, I would have taken it off. I don't know how I missed him! But Robbie Turner was following up, and he put it in. We ended up beating them 3-1.

We had played a couple of non-League sides, and beat them, then we got Swindon, when Ossie Ardiles was manager – a big match for us in the West Country — and we beat them 2-1, and in the end we went out to Cambridge United. We drew 0-0 at our place, 1-1 in Cambridge, and then we tossed a coin, lost, and had to play at their place again. And they beat us 5-1. That's when Dion Dublin and Turner were playing, just bombing the ball up front to them. And all the tricks from John Beck – the sugar in the tea, and the cold

Bob in classic pose, as he scores another goal in City's 4-2 win against Blackburn

23

water, and turning up the heating in the dressing room, and the noise. It was a good cup run while it lasted, but the main thing was the League." Bob's favourite goal for City was an overhead kick in a 1-0 win against Birmingham City that season.

Sadly, it all started to go wrong against Crewe at Ashton Gate on April 10. "What was a shame that season, was that I missed the last eight games. I'd already scored 34 goals in 37 games, and people were saying I might get forty. The last game I played, when I was carried off on a stretcher, with a hamstring injury, was against Crewe, and I scored a hat-trick before I was injured." It definitely upset the team. "We had a couple of defeats, and I'm not saying it was because I got injured, but of course, I'd been in a real purple patch after Christmas, scoring a lot of goals, so it made a difference, and we didn't score as regularly."

Without Bob in the side, Rovers gradually caught up, and their 3-0 win over City in the penultimate game of the season, at Twerton Park, won the championship for the Gasheads. City still won automatic promotion, but it was a big disappointment, missing out on the championship to such hated local rivals.

"The rivalry in Bristol is awesome. It's like the one here, the Black Country Derby. I mean, having two teams in one city, especially one of that size. Rovers were a supported club, but with Twerton Park only having a capacity of six or seven thousand, in was a sell-out week-in, week-out. They were the Gasheads, and they called the City fans the Shitheads. If you ask Rovers players who they played for, they'll tell you they played for the Gas – whilst me and Gary Shelton, who's here

Bob collects his Golden Boot Award at Ashton Gate in 1990

24

at the Albion now, will say we played for the Shits! It was always intense, and we had some good ding-dong battles with them. But I could never score against them, except in the Gloucestershire Senior Cup Final, when I put two goals past Nigel Martyn in a pre-season game."

1990 was a very special year for Bob. He was named as City's *Player of the Year* at the end of the season, and on June 2, he had a very special match of his own – when he married Lesley. The couple set up home in a lovely suburb of Weston-super-Mare. "And my daughter Chantelle was born April 21 1991, so she was a honeymoon baby, I think!"

City – and Bob – got off to an excellent start to their Second Division campaign in August 1990, Taylor scoring twice in a 4-2 home win over Blackburn Rovers, in front of over 13,000 fans. By now, though, Joe Jordan was no longer in charge. "By then Joe had become a bit of a commodity in the football world, and had been

Bob tangles in the snow with future colleague Graham Roberts — City won 2-0

tempted away to Scotland by Hearts, who were a big club at the time. Jimmy Lumsden – a former Leeds United man – had taken over and he was the manager at the start of the new season."

In the first round of the Rumbelows Cup, City were drawn against the Albion, and they managed a creditable 2-2 draw in the first leg at The Hawthorns. In the second leg, it was a different story, as Albion dominated the game, but could not score in the normal ninety minutes. The game hinged on an incident in the 16th minute of extra time, when Gary Strodder was sent off for a clattering tackle from behind on Taylor; six minutes later, Smith scored City's winner, and Albion were lucky to end the tie with ten men on the pitch, for Daryl Burgess should surely have been sent off for a blatant professional foul on Taylor, who came in for some pretty hefty treatment from his future colleagues. There was more, ten days later, as City lost 2-1 in the League at The Hawthorns; a shove in the back from Strodder, clearly still annoyed from the previous meeting, saw Bob win a penalty – only for Stuart Naylor to save from Aizelwood.

That was City's first defeat of the season; it was then that their season fell away. At the start of October they stood fifth in the Second Division, in a Play-off spot that could have seen them regain a place in the top flight that they had lost in 1980, and they had just won 1-0 at Roker Park in their second round first leg Rumbelows Cup tie against First Division Sunderland. On October 3 they lost 3-0 at Filbert Street. Three days later they lost 4-0 to Wolves at Molineux – conceding a Steve Bull hat-trick — and then, incredibly, they lost their second leg game against Sunderland 6-1 at Ashton Gate.

Bob never really regained his form of the previous season, and on a number of occasions only made it onto the substitutes' bench. One match he did score in, though, was the game against the Albion at Ashton Gate, on February 2, which City won 2-0. Bob scored the second City goal – only his fifth of the campaign — in the 60th minute. "I remember it well. I made a run, turned Graham Roberts and put it into the bottom corner. I can remember it because it was on the snow, and we had to play with an orange ball."

Seventeen minutes later, just as in the cup-tie, undisciplined Albion had a man sent off, when Paul Raven deliberately stamped on Nicky Morgan's chest. That lack of discipline would see Albion relegated to the Third Division at the end of the season. Bob ended the campaign with just eleven goals, all scored in the League as City – who had got as high as fifth in early March – staged a late rally to end in ninth place, just one win from a Play-off place.

The Albion — and Bobby Gould

Bob started what would prove to be his final season at Bristol City with a goal, the equaliser in a 1-1 draw against Southend United at Roots Hall on the season's opening day. By now he had lost his number nine shirt, which was firmly in the possession of lanky centre-forward Wayne Allison, who would end the season as City's top scorer, albeit with just ten goals. Bob's overall total would exceed that – but not all of them would be scored in the red number ten shirt of Bristol City. "That season we seemed to have a load of strikers; Nicky Morgan, Leroy Rosenior, me, Robbie Turner and Terry Connor. There was a glut of strikers, and I always seemed to be in the reserves."

After twice being substituted in the games that followed the Southend game, Bob was dropped for the big Derby game with Bristol Rovers at Ashton Gate on September 4. City won that one 1-0 in front of their biggest gate of the season, to maintain their unbeaten start to the new campaign, but their form slumped again, with a League Cup defeat by Rovers following, and Bob earned a recall from the Reserves for the visit of Newcastle United on October 26. He came up trumps with another late equaliser in a 1-1 draw in front of just 8,613 fans.

Back in the side, Bob would score just two more goals for City, in a 3-1 defeat at Ayresome Park, and, to salvage yet another late point, in a 1-1 draw at home to Swindon, on Boxing Day. Sixteen days later, Taylor played his last game for City, substituted by Nicky Morgan in the second half of a terrible 4-0 mauling by Blackburn Rovers at Ewood Park. City manager Jimmy Lumsden was coming in for severe criticism for his side's poor form – they would go eighteen games with just one win – and he decided to raise cash for new players by selling Bob to another manager who was also struggling to satisfy his club's supporters, a division below. City had just broken their transfer record by paying Celtic £250,000 for Polish international striker Jacki Dziekanowski, and Taylor was one of City's few saleable assets. Lumsden would lose his job a matter of weeks after Bob's departure, replaced by one of Taylor's future managers, Denis Smith. Ironically, with the money received for Taylor, Smith would later sign a hot young prospect from Arsenal – Andy Cole...

Bob failed to rate Lumsden as ideal for the job from the start. "I never looked on Jimmy as manager material. He was a good assistant-manager, always in the dressing room, having a cup of tea and a bet with the lads, friendly with the players. He was probably too close to us, so when he got the job he had to distance himself, and it didn't really work. He'd always been praising me as a striker before that, but when he was in charge, he dropped me a few times."

Bobby Gould's decision to sign Bob Taylor from Bristol City stretched back to December 1991 when he had been forced – against his will – to sell his star striker, Don Goodman, to Sunderland. In purely financial terms, the sale had been a good bit of business, making a clear profit of £900,000 on a player who had cost just £50,000 from Bradford City less than five years before. The cash input had wiped out Albion's worrying overdraft, as chairman John Silk had tried to explain at the time to Albion's angry fans. "This was a time when sound business sense was needed. We consulted Bobby, and he did not want to sell Goodman. That is natural; but he is also a realist, and knew it was common sense. There is no way he wants to be manager of a club in jeopardy."

When Albion sold Goodman, on the eve of an Autoglass Trophy game at Lincoln, they were riding high in the Third Division, and still in the FA Cup. By the end of January, they had been eliminated from both cup competitions, by Exeter and Orient, respectively, and their League form was beginning to suffer. The crisis came to a head on Saturday January 25, with the visit of Swansea City to The Hawthorns. City were a poor side, and Albion soon raced into a two goal lead – only for Swansea to score three times in the last twelve minutes to grab a stunning victory. Hundreds of fans stopped behind on the Birmingham Road terraces at the final whistle, to protest at John Silk and Bobby Gould, and it was not until 6pm that they drifted away, past a convoy of police reinforcements waiting silently outside in Halfords Lane. They went then only after an impassioned plea from Gould, in front of the Brummie Road. Armed with a microphone he said, "The buck stops with me and the players," before answering questions and telling fans he had £250,000 to spend on players. Gould was as good as his word. Forty-eight hours later, Albion announced a press conference to show off their new signing, as Gould broke the bank to spend £300,000 on Bob Taylor.

Bob was keen to move on at that period in his career. "That was a bad time for me. My Mum had died in the November, and I went through a bit of a bad time, because, well, you know, your Mum's your Mum. Living in Bristol, I was so far away that I hadn't got to see my Mum that much recently, so it was particularly upsetting. At the end of the day, you look back, and think, 'Well, a change is as good as a rest' — and you move. The day after Bobby Gould approached me, I spoke to him, and agreed to move to the Albion. That's the way I was – a spur of the moment thing, and I just went for it. Jimmy came in to see me and told me that Bobby Gould had been on the phone, and that they'd offered £300,000. I said yes straightaway."

This was after he had made a few enquiries about his prospective new employers. "Now, Johnny Giles had been manager at the Albion not long before, and at City one of the apprentices was Chris Giles, his youngest son. I asked him about the Albion. 'Oh, you don't want to go to that place. It's a shit-hole. They treat everybody shite, they don't spend money, they're crap.' Even after those words of wisdom, I came up, spoke to Bobby, spoke to Lesley, because we'd just had Chantelle then, and I said OK. It was all done and dusted overnight. I had two days training, and then made my debut against Brentford."

Gould, naturally enough, was highly enthusiastic about his new capture, as he remembered years later. "I was living in the West Country and saw him play loads of times; I thought he was a natural predator who would always score goals. He always knew where the ball was going to drop, and you can't coach that into players. I nicked him for £300,000. And I dovetailed him with Gary Robson, which worked really well. And as a person he was as sound as a pound – a solid lad who would always give his best."

Bobby Gould, Manager of the Month

It was not the first time that Gould had watched Taylor. "When Bobby was selling the club to me, he told me that he'd been watching me when he was at Wimbledon, and that he'd always fancied me as a player, that he'd just sold Don Goodman, and needed a striker who could score goals. I suppose it was exactly what I wanted to hear – that somebody wanted me, after being a bit out of it at Bristol. I got a few letters from City fans, thanking me. They sold me against the wishes of the fans, but if I had stayed, I might have damaged the relationship that I had with the fans, so perhaps it was as well. And I think I needed a new challenge – a big kick up the arse, in fact. People don't know you at the new club, and you have to make an impression, and it's a fresh start. And it was an hour and a half nearer the north-east!"

Not that Bob moved house for quite some time. "Of course, for quite a while I had to commute from Weston to the Albion. The following season, I'd come up and stay at weekends with a big mate of mine, Gary Robson, as well as the Moat House at times. When I first arrived at the Albion, the first players I met were Graham Roberts and Stewart Bowen – they were making a bit of money selling shell-suits to the rest of the lads!" Garry Bannister, who had been guilty of several glaring misses against the Swans, was the unlucky man to make way for Bob to make his Albion debut against the Third Division leaders at The Hawthorns, on Saturday February 1.

And what a debut that was, as Bob was immediately taken to the hearts of the Albion fans with a goal after just eleven minutes. Graham Roberts won possession with a bone-shattering intervention on the half way line, Gary Robson collected the ball and put through a delightful lobbed pass which beat the offside trap, and allowed Taylor to score a goal with a well-placed low shot, which went in off the body of the advancing keeper, at the Birmingham Road end. The celebrations were completed with a second goal from Wayne Fereday, as Albion completed a League 'Double' over the West London side, having already won 2-1 at Griffin Park.

SuperBob scores on his debut against Brentford at The Hawthorns

If that was a good start, it was as nothing compared to his feat the following week, when Albion took on rivals Birmingham City at St Andrews. Up to that point, Bob had not been too successful in local Derbies at Bristol. "Rovers were always my bogey side. I never knew what it was like to score in a big Derby game in Bristol. I got two in a Gloucestershire Cup game before the start of this season, but that hardly counts, so it would be nice to get off the mark straight away against the Blues." Bob needn't have worried. In front of a crowd of 27,508 – Blues' biggest League attendance for four years, and, indeed, the biggest attendance in Division Three that season – Albion got off to a great start. They were always well in control even before Trevor Matthewson's twelfth minute dismissal for an off-the-ball elbow on Gary Robson. Robson got his revenge with the opening goal – and then Bob took over.

Two minutes before half time Wayne Fereday collected a pass from Roberts and fired at goal; Alan Miller, the on-loan Arsenal keeper who would one day be a colleague of Taylor's at The Hawthorns, could only parry the shot, and when the ball spun up into the air, Taylor was there first to score with a spectacular diving header. In the 71st minute he scored his second, when he nipped in, in front of Miller at the near post, to scoop full-back Graham Harbey's left wing cross over the line. Never again would Bob have any problems scoring in Derby games, and he and the fans would celebrate many a winner against both the Blues and the Wolves...

Bob celebrates after scoring his second goal at St Andrews

31

"At the end of that game big John Gayle clattered Gary Robson, and I can remember Graham Roberts — who isn't that big, really — going up to him and giving such verbal abuse, and Gayley apologising, saying, "I'm sorry Robbo, it's my head man, it's in a mess. I don't know what I'm doing!"

It was unfortunate that Albion would only hold the leadership for four days, for on the following Wednesday they went down by a solitary goal to bogey side Stoke City, who leapfrogged over the Albion to take pole position. "The game that really did it for us, was the defeat at Stoke. It was only one setback, but after that Bobby kept bringing in new faces, and swapping the team about, and it all went wrong. After that, the animosity was there, and you could feel the hate between the fans and the manager, and the board. Once I'd settled down, after a few weeks, I began to rue not taking Chris Giles' advice, some of the things that were going on!"

Taylor's next goal would come two weeks later, a last minute consolation goal in a 2-1 defeat at Bournemouth, but Bob would remember the game for an extraordinary incident which took place after the game. "We were in the dressing room after the game, and we'd lost 2-1 – I'd scored a late goal. We were in the dressing room, with these big glass windows, and we could see this big silhouette outside, and there was this chap outside, giving us a right bollocking. Bobby tip-toed out and dragged in this Mick Coldicott, and told him to give us a bollocking to our faces! And he did. He was saying something and Graham Roberts jumped up and said 'Don't you

Bob scores at Bournemouth — then gets abused by a fan in the dressing room!

****ing tell me what I can and can't do – who do you think you are!' And at the end of it, Gouldy told him he wanted him to give us the pre-match team talk before the next home game, against Torquay. Incredible! The papers got wind of it, of course, and made a big thing of it."

Mick Coldicott recalled the incident. "They were rubbish. I had a few words with some of them, and told them what I thought. You might as well get eleven people off Smethwick High Street if that's the best they can do. I took a day off work to watch the game; I wondered whether it was worth it," said Coldicott. "The players gave as good as they got," retorted Gould afterwards. As Bob remembered, "Back he came the following week, and the first person he met was Robbo, who said, 'And don't ****ing think you'll be saying anything to me!' That deflated him, so all he said then was 'Oh, go out there and play well lads, that's your team talk!' Short and sweet, like..."

Perhaps it had an effect, although it is difficult not to wonder what 17-year old debutant YTS midfielder Roy Hunter made of it all. Maybe he thought that bringing in a supporter to harangue the team was normal procedure. In any event, Hunter scored a debut goal as Albion won 1-0 in a tempestuous game that saw three men sent off, two of them from the visitors' side, including their assistant player-manager, and former Norwich star Justin Fashanu, as well as Albion's Darren Bradley.

Generally speaking, though, it was not a good atmosphere in which to try to play good football. "There were all sorts of things going on at that time. There was the incident during training, in the boxing ring, when Bobby got in, put the gloves on, and asked anybody if they wanted to box him. Colin West got in the ring, put on the gloves – and just smacked him in the mouth, cut him all up. And Bobby managed to keep his dignity, and said 'And that's what you get if you don't keep your defences up!'"

Even football training could be a bizarre experience. "We used to do these five or six corners in training a short corner, far post corner, and so on — and I remember we got a corner once in a League game at The Hawthorns, and I looked round and Bobby was actually holding up one of the old number boards that they used for substitutes, holding up a '3' so we would do 'corner number 3!' Then there was 'Mongo.' Darren Bradley would go out, put his foot on the ball at a free kick, and shout 'Mongo.' We'd get ready to run, and then he'd shout 'Double Mongo' and all but one of us would run forward, and the defenders were supposed to follow us, and leave a gap at the back. I think it actually worked once, and we got a goal from it... There were lots of strange things like that."

Two weeks after the dressing room fiasco, Bob got the chance to see first hand exactly what the fans thought of the Gould regime, when they staged another demonstration at The Hawthorns following a dismal 3-2 defeat by Leyton Orient. Albion actually played a lot better against Orient than they had done against Torquay, but the defeat was a serious setback to Albion's hopes of automatic promotion. More than five hundred fans remained after the game, calling for the chairman's head, with police and stewards standing and watching as the fans congregated at the back of the Birmingham Road end. Superintendent Dave Craddock, of West Bromwich police, described the incident as "a totally peaceful protest" with no arrests.

There was yet another protest after the next home game, when Albion missed out on the chance of pulling to within a point of the top two by losing disastrously — of all clubs — to Hartlepool United. This time 400 people stopped behind after the game, calling for Gould's head and an appearance from the players, and singing "Haven't we had enough?" Police patience wore thin after half an hour, when the fans were shepherded to the exits.

Gould, for once, denied the press entry to the dressing room after the game. "I'm responsible, I'm top of the ship. I have got to take the brickbats as well as the plaudits; but promotion is still very much a reality." In fact, the game was the start of a slide which would see Albion finish even outside the Play-off positions. The season lurched further when, the day before the game at Bury, Bobby

Albion assistant manager Stuart Pearson

Gould decided to 'suspend' his assistant manager, Stuart Pearson, for 'disloyalty.' Pearson announced he would sue the club for wrongful dismissal if the board backed Gould and sacked him. "If I'm the one to lose out, then I'd be left with no option but to defend my reputation and sue, either the club or Bobby Gould," said Pearson.

Before the game at Gigg Lane, Albion's two thousand travelling supporters started up a chant of 'Stuart Pearson's Blue and White Army' after hearing the news of the assistant manager's suspension by Gould. Gould also rang the changes in the team, dropping Bradley, McNally, Robson, Fereday and Bannister (Roberts was out injured for the rest of the season) and bringing in Paul Raven, Craig Shakespeare, Neil Cartwright, Paul Williams, Winston White and, for his League debut, young Carl Heggs, fresh from his loan spell at Stafford Rangers. Albion gained a point in their first League visit to Bury in over forty years, when Bob scored a spectacular scissor kick in the ninth minute, to equalise an earlier goal from Mark Kearney, but dropped down another place in the table.

Bob's next goal was in a location somewhat more glamorous than Bury's Graveyard End – he scored in Albion's 4-0 friendly win at the Victoria Stadium, in Gibraltar. "Gibraltar was actually the first footballing trip I ever went on. Gouldy put curfews on, but he didn't stop the lads enjoying themselves. We played one

Bob scores a late equaliser against one of his favourite sides — Bolton Wanderers

game, on Astroturf, and we won 4-0, with me and Gary Robson starting off up front, and we both scored goals. Gouldy was all right, and the lads went out and had a couple of beers, but I think it got a bit out of hand. They sneaked back in, and there was a bit of a rumpus at the hotel one night, and some pots got broken. So we had a meeting on the roof-top the following morning, and he threatened us – 'If anything like that happens again, you're straight off home,' but it was OK after that."

By the time the Albion party returned from the Mediterranean, the board had sacked Pearson, and Gould was on his own. "There was more strange stuff with Stuart Pearson – 'Pancho.' He was a striker, and he was great for me, and gave me some good advice. But I don't really know what happened there. I'd only just arrived, and Gouldy came in one morning and told us all, 'I've got rid of him as well, because he's been stabbing me in the back as well.' But I have no idea what had been going on, and, to be honest, I didn't want to know, because I didn't want to get involved in it."

Gould was not to last very much longer. Successive 3-0 defeats at Huddersfield and Stockport left Albion well out of touch with the leading clubs, in eighth place, needing a win at closest rivals Peterborough. In a poor goalless draw, Albion's best chance came in the last minute, when Bob Taylor, of all people, was left completely in the clear, ten yards out, but as he

The infamous 'coffin demonstration' at Shrewsbury's Gay Meadow

swivelled onto the ball, he put it past the post. In injury time, Paul Williams was sent off, farcically, for abusing the linesman over a decision about the position of his feet when taking a throw-in.

Albion still clung on forlornly to their Play-off hopes, which were finally extinguished with another dismal defeat at Booth-ferry Park. The season ended with a win at Shrewsbury, but the circumstances were unsavoury. Before the game against the already relegated Shrews, hundreds of Albion fans paraded through the town, carrying coffins and effigies of Bobby Gould, as it was generally known that it would be the hated manager's last game. "Bobby was generally a straight-talking bloke. He was great with me, he signed me, and he was always honest with me. The last nail in his coffin – literally, because the Albion fans were carrying a coffin with his name on before the game – was at Shrewsbury, on the last day of the season."

Bob remembers the day well; and one incident in particular. "We had been stopping in a hotel in the town centre before the game, so instead of going there by bus, we had to walk the

Bob has to admit it; sometimes even he plays pants...

half mile or so to the ground, down the big hill, across the bridge, and through the fans. We were getting so much abuse, but Bobby walked out right in front of us, and we dragged behind, and left him on his own. The coffin was there, and they were slagging him off so much. I can remember going across this little bridge, and going past a chippie. There was this bloke in the queue, and he was so angry that he went right up to Bobby, and eyeballed him. "You ****ing so-and-so, we don't want you, why don't you go and **** off!" And Bobby just stood there and took it. I don't know if the guy had run out of stuff to say, or was just too embarrassed, or just was so shocked because Gouldy had stared him out, but he just stopped in his tracks, moved out of the way, and Gould walked on. Maybe he was looking for a reaction – but he didn't get one, and that impressed me with Gouldy. He just walked on through the crowd." There was a touch of the absurd amongst all the anger. "There was all that hate around – and we just walked out onto the pitch in sun-glasses and t-shirts and Bermuda shorts! It was a Beachwear Party, and we had to throw the glasses and t-shirts into the crowd."

Ironically, his side gave their best performance of the campaign, with Bob putting them three goals up at half time with his twelfth League goal of the season (including four for Bristol City). Two minutes before time, the huge crowd at the Albion end of the quaint little stadium invaded the pitch, refusing to leave and looking out for Bobby Gould, who had wisely left the dug-out to seek safety in the main stand. The mob broke the crossbar and police were still battling to clear the pitch when the PA system announced that the game had indeed finished, two minutes short of the ninety. The referee, however, was adamant that the match had not been abandoned. "I have discussed the matter with the police and no matter what anyone thinks, 90 minutes had elapsed when I blew the final whistle. What happened after that will not be included in my report."

And still the humiliation was not over. Just 24 hours after the unpleasantness at Gay Meadow, the supporters staged the *Player of the Year* Night at the King's Theatre in Great Barr. Gould was still manager, although expected to be sacked at any time, but after taking twenty minutes of sarcastic abuse from the MC, WM Sports reporter Malcolm Boyden, he stormed out of the hall, picking up the microphone to say "I apologise for what is happening. I don't mind criticism for myself, but not for my players." Boyden made several references to the fact that Gould was believed to be negotiating with Coventry City for a return to Highfield Road, but the comment which finally made Gould explode was when Boyden produced a velvet bag containing all the players' names. "This is how we'll choose the *Player of the Year*, because this is how the Albion team has been selected all season."

Bob was stunned by it all. "The *Player of The Year* Night was different to what I'd ever experienced before anyway – at Bristol it had just been a small thing in the John Atyeo Suite at the club. This time was a big thing, with the wives there, at the Kings Theatre in Hamstead. Malcolm Boyden came on and did a stint. He was hammering the manager and the chairman. He was singing a sarcastic song, and went right up to the chairman's face and sang it to him. That was all too much for Gouldy, and he got up and stormed out, and we all followed him. As we went out, he told us all to meet him at The Hawthorns, for a good drink. I can remember the fans all standing up asking us not to go. I just got up and followed the crowd. I couldn't believe it."

A number of players – particularly those who had already fallen out with Gould — including Colin West, Roberts, Hackett and McNally, returned later to chat to some of the five hundred amazed fans. Boyden later apologised. "If I went over the top, then I apologise. All I was trying to do was to keep everything light-hearted."

On Tuesday May 5, Gould was sacked and John Silk, who had initially opposed Gould's appointment, fell on his sword, stepping down as chairman, although remaining as a director. The new chairman was local wood-worker, Trevor Summers, earlier nicknamed by former manager Ron Atkinson as 'Trev the Shed.' Sensationally, on May 8, the board appointed 39-year old Argentinian World Cup hero Ossie Ardiles as their new manager, ahead of other candidates in the frame, Stuart Pearson, Archie Gemmill, Terry Cooper, Bruce Rioch, Alan Buckley, Ray Harford, Mel Machin, Ian Bowyer, Brian Horton and John Rudge.

Ardiles immediately brought in former Spurs manager Keith Burkinshaw, who had initially brought Ardiles – and Ricky Villa – over from South America in 1978, as his assistant. Ardiles soon set how he intended his side to play. "My philosophy is simple. We pass the ball to a player wearing the same colour shirt, and run hard to win the ball when we haven't got it. It's a system designed to score goals, because without goals, you don't win matches. Swindon were the Second Division's highest goalscorers when we won promotion in 1990. My team also scored regularly at Newcastle, but we also conceded too many goals as well. That experience has taught me some valuable lessons."

Within days Ardiles had taken a knife to Albion's playing squad, releasing Graham Roberts, Colin West, Stewart Bowen, Darren Rogers, Steve Parkin, David Pritchard, Les Palmer, and Adrian Foster.

Bob remembers that period because of the uncertainty for many of the players. "At the end of that season they got Ossie Ardiles in, and we had to wait, to stay behind after the end of the season for an extra two weeks, and we were playing five-a-side every day across the pitch at The Hawthorns. That was the period when he had players into his office and told them whether he wanted them or not, and he got rid of Westy, Graham Roberts, and quite a few others.

Then we were sent away on holiday. Before we went Ossie told us about how he wanted to play attacking football. Keith Burkinshaw, the surly one, chalk and cheese alongside Ossie, just said 'I'll see you all in pre-season. Make sure you're ready for it, because it's going to be a hard one.' We all thought, 'Oh no!'"

Ossie Ardiles and his assistant, Keith Burkinshaw, soon after taking over at the Albion

Ossie from Tottingham

The players assembled apprehensively for pre-season training, in July 1992, wondering exactly what was going to happen to them. They needn't have worried. "The start of the following season we were training on the old Mitchells & Butler ground. Ossie brought in a fitness specialist and we had a seven minute run, at pace, round the M&B, on that first day. And that was the last we saw of him. Ossie said to us, 'No, it's too much – we don't want that sort of training.' And that was that! All we did was short, sharp stuff, and loads of five-a-sides. Ossie was very football-orientated – he was much more interested in the passing side of things rather than the fitness. One touch, two touch practice games. Then we'd have two players in the middle and we'd have to keep the ball off them; if they were in the middle for twenty passes, then they'd have to pay a pound each into the kitty. We did that for an hour every day – and it was a great laugh. A bit of team work, then a quick five-a-side game – it was a lovely time."

Bob had the greatest respect for his new manager. "Ossie kept his distance, but he also knew how to look after the lads. You could go into his office and talk to him as well – if you could understand a word he was saying, that is! I think that maybe we should have done a lot better for him than we did in the League in the end." Bob got off to a great start – even in the pre-season friendlies, of which there were many, as Ardiles tried to instil his attacking ethos into the team right from the start. He scored in all of the first four games that Albion played, at Evesham, Hereford, St Albans and – against Premier opposition – at home to Sheffield Wednesday.

By the time the League season started, Ardiles had blooded in his three new signings, Ian Hamilton, Steve Lilwall and, as a partner for Taylor, experienced striker Simon Garner, a former colleague of the Argentinian, briefly, at Blackburn, and Albion hit the ground running, with a 3-1 opening day home win. "I scored twice in the first game of the season, against Blackpool. We went in front, then young Roy Hunter gave them a goal from a back pass – it was the first day of the new back pass rule. I scored with a header to put us in front again, then I scored with a volley. Not a bad start!" Indeed, it was a great start to what would be a great season. Ardiles' men would not just be merely successful – they would be successful in style, winning friends all over the country, scoring loads of goals (ironically, second only to Ardiles' former club, Newcastle, now managed by Kevin Keegan) and thrilling their long-suffering fans.

And chiefly responsible for most of those goals was SuperBob, as he surpassed his previous best at Bristol City, and ended the campaign with 37 goals in League, FA, Coca Cola and Autoglass cups.

Not that Bob failed to see the parallel between his spells at the two clubs. "It's strange the way that everything I did at Bristol City was mirrored at the Albion. At both clubs I came in at the end of one season, scored eight goals in a short spell, then the following season, I got nearly forty goals each time. Then I had a bit of a barren spell, at Bristol and, later, at the Albion, and moved on. It's uncanny, really."

Bob was on target again, in the midweek game following the Blackpool match, as Albion beat Plymouth – who Ardiles had turned down to become Albion boss — in the Coca Cola Cup. Bob scored the only goal of the game, with a fizzing header from a McNally free kick, but his greatest satisfaction came from the fact that he had beaten the great Peter Shilton, Plymouth's player-manager. "It was quite a thrill, just like when I beat Grobbelaar at Leeds. Peter was past his best, but he was still a great keeper – and he saved a penalty from Hammy late in the game." That penalty miss would prove expensive, as Albion went down 2-0 in the second leg, to take an early exit from the cup once again.

Albion shrugged off the disappointment of their early cup exit at Home Park by racking up a splendid unbeaten opening sequence of seven games in the League. In the home game against high-riding Bournemouth, Bob headed the first goal that the south coast side had conceded all season, then, late in the game, won the penalty that Craig Shakespeare put away to win the game. Unusually, in the next game, at home to fellow challengers Stockport, Bob was forced to take a subsidiary role to his striking partner, Simon Garner, who plundered two goals in a comfortable 3-0 win, that saw Albion at the top of the Second Division – this was the season that the divisions were 'renumbered' after the creation of the Premier League.

Bob was back on target in the 1-1 draw at Fulham, and scored two more in another easy win over Reading, but it was his two goals at title favourites Bolton that really made people take notice of Albion's challenge. The home side had won all their games so far at Burnden Park, and dominated a goalless first half, only to miss a string of chances.

Ten minutes into the second half, Bob headed a classic goal from Stacey Coldicott's cross. Seven minutes from time, even though he was limping from a bad challenge, he topped that with a wonderful scissors kick from a Gary Hackett cross. Bob always made a good impression against Bolton, something which would be of great significance later in his career. He was already causing waves. Peter Reid, the Manchester City boss, and his chief scout, Ian Greaves, were both watching Bob, but Ardiles was quick to scotch the transfer rumours. "We are selling nobody – especially Bob Taylor," declared Ardiles. "His finishing is in a different class."

Four days later came one of the classic games of the season, when Albion, unbeaten in the League, took on Stoke City, at the Victoria Ground. It was a fascinating contrast of styles, with Ardiles' push and run style up against the more brutal direct approach favoured by Stoke boss Lou Macari, accompanied by an offside trap that stopped Albion repeatedly. In a real see-saw game, Albion took the lead against the run of play, when Stoke

Bob in classic pose, after scoring at Stoke City

keeper, Tony Parks, who was making his Stoke debut, miskicked a goal kick straight to Taylor, who controlled the ball, ran in on goal, rounded the keeper, and scored a super goal.

In quick succession, Albion lost both of their full-backs to injury – and nearly lost a third, when substitute Wayne Fereday, filling in at left back, pulled a thigh muscle, but bravely battled on. Just before the interval, Stoke equalised, and a minute into the second half, took the lead – the first time that Albion had been behind in the League all season.

Albion absorbed a considerable amount of pressure, before Bob equalised in the 70th minute, with a great header from a Fereday cross, and three minutes later Bob turned provider to set up Garner to score with an angled drive that saw Albion 3-2 ahead.

Albion were ahead this time for all of two minutes, and seven minutes from the end, Ian Cranson – brother of Geoff Cranson, Bob's coach at Horden Colliery – scored the goal that sent Albion down to an undeserved first defeat of the season.

For a while – a very short while – the goals dried up for Bob, as he went four games without scoring. Not surprisingly, that was Bob's – and Albion's – worst spell of the season, as they lost three of those four games, to slip – permanently – off the top of the table. Bob got back into scoring mode in the 2-2 draw at home to Rotherham, but it took a fluke last minute goal from midfielder Darren Bradley to get Albion back on the winning track against Hull at Boothferry Park. That was followed by a comfortable 3-1 home win

Bob hits the net again, this time with a penalty at Bradford's Valley Parade

44

against Hartlepool, when Bob had a new striking partner, for Ardiles had signed former England international Luther Blissett on loan from Watford. Blissett scored the third goal that evening, to add to an earlier one from Bob, who thus scored against the side he had once been associated with as a youngster. It was his twelfth goal of the season.

There was a great chance for Bob to add to that goal tally, when Albion were drawn at home to non-League outfit Aylesbury United, in the first round of the FA Cup. Not that Albion were comfortable against such opposition, even though they had beaten Marlow 6-0 the year before; in 1991, infamously, they had been humiliated at The Hawthorns by Woking, and Albion supporters will be forever wary of such under-rated sides.

This time, though, there was no mistake, as rampant Albion rattled in eight goals – their best win in the Cup for over a century. "We won 8-0. I scored one, but it should have been two. I'd beaten the keeper to a header, and Ian Hamilton stopped it on the line. You can see me on the video, giving him a bollocking. 'Hammy, you ****!' 'I'm sorry Bob, I couldn't get out of the way.' 'Get out of the way? It was going in!' It was just like the Brendan Ormsby goal all over again. But I thought he was offside as well, and they were going to disallow it. I was desperate to score after that, in such a big win, and I got another looping header that Hammy very wisely kept away from! Kevin Donovan completed his hat-trick with a great goal that he lobbed over the keeper. A lovely goal." Young Kevin Donovan had been brought in for a song from Huddersfield Town, and, for all his inexperience, became a vital member of that promotion side, and a good foil for Bob.

Albion still had serious problems in the League; three draws and a defeat – at rivals Leyton Orient – meant that they had slipped as low as fourth in a Second Division that was being dominated by the two Potteries clubs, Port Vale and Stoke, the latter having climbed to top spot with an inspired unbeaten run.

Things were looking up in the Cup, at least, when Albion took on another non-league side, Wycombe Wanderers, managed by Martin O'Neill, and raced into a two goal lead at Adams Park. Bob scored the second, and, not long after, hit the underside of the crossbar when presented with the opportunity to 'kill off' the tie. Instead, Wycombe fought back and scored twice in the last quarter of an hour to earn a money-spinning replay at The Hawthorns.

That tie caused controversy, when the Albion board recommended that Bobby Gould, who had been *Sky* TV's summariser in the first game, stay away from The Hawthorns because they could not guarantee his safety. The tie was another thriller, and at times Albion rode their luck, before Bob popped up, nine minutes from time, to earn a home third round tie against West Ham.

"We'd lost a two goal lead at Wycombe because 'Bruiser' – keeper Stuart Naylor – had broken his hand, and let in a soft goal, because he couldn't use his hand. The replay at The Hawthorns was live on *Sky* as well, and then the pressure really was on, because everybody expects an upset. And we could have lost it. But I scored a late winner – and I was really pleased with it, one of the best goals I've ever scored with my left foot, drilled right into the corner, with a bit of bend on it!"

Bob would go another four games without a goal before getting off the mark in the Autoglass Trophy game against Walsall at The Hawthorns. Early in the game, Craig Shakespeare missed a penalty, his second such recent miss. When Bob won another spot-kick late in the game, he took it himself – and scored the first penalty of his career. That game – a 4-0 win — also saw the debut of an odd Taylor goal celebration – a touching of wrist and ankles with reserve player Carl Heggs — that was to become a feature of the latter part of the campaign. "I don't know what that was. We saw all these other players doing these celebrations, and Heggsey was always going on, 'If I could get a game, I'd score a goal and I'd do this and I'd do that...' So I said to him, 'If you play and score your first senior goal, then we'll do a celebration.' I don't know whether I saw

Bob and Carl Heggs devise their very own goalscoring celebration

it somewhere else, but we were supposed to do it three times, then wave our hands about. Heggsey did it twice, and I did it three times, by which time Carl had already started waggling his hands, so it looked really stupid! We had to work on it a bit after that..."

A week later, Bob scored again in the same competition; or did he? In their second — and meaningless, because the four goals against Walsall had already assured their qualification — tie at Field Mill, Albion beat Mansfield Town 1-0, and Bob scored the only goal, a header at the far post. "I did – I headed the ball, I know I did. But I've looked at the video loads of times, and you can't tell whether it's me or Marc Sinfield." Most people in the sparse attendance at Field Mill that night gave the goal to the young debutant defender, as he and Taylor jumped for the cross together, but Bob claimed it, and it went down in the records as one of a total of 37 that season.

As Albion moved into the second half of the season, they bowed out of the FA Cup against First Division West Ham, which at least left them free to concentrate on the Second Division promotion race – with the Autoglass Trophy as a possible route to Wembley. Three vital games, which helped decide the whole season, took place in January. On the 9th, Albion took on a Bolton side that had been storming up the table after a slow start, and who were unbeaten for fifteen games. It was the Trotters who took an early lead, from the penalty spot, but Albion fought back brilliantly, with Bob scoring the third and clinching goal in the 71st minute. Incredibly, it was

Bob's — or Marc's — it's difficult to tell, in the Autoglass game at Field Mill

47

Bob's first League goal since November 3; but it was to herald the start of another great scoring run.

But not immediately. The following week, Albion travelled to play Exeter City at St James Park, a game that was generally recognised as a turning point for the whole season. In the first half, Albion were truly abysmal. Paul Raven scored an own goal and should have conceded a penalty, but the referee missed his blatant handball in the box. Even so, with twenty minutes remaining, Albion were two goals down, and promotion was looking a distant dream. Then, with Raven off and Ian Hamilton drawn back as a sweeper, Carl Heggs scored his first League goal, to give Albion some hope. A Taylor header was collected by Gary Hackett, who scored his only goal of the season to level, and seven minutes from the end, the game ended in real drama. A long boot from Stuart Naylor ran right through to Bob, who ran though on goal, only to be brutally chopped down by goalkeeper Kevin Miller.

Referee George Ashby sent the keeper off, and awarded a penalty. Bob, who had become the club's *de facto* penalty taker after failures by Craig Shakespeare, Bernard McNally and Ian Hamilton, was still receiving treatment off the pitch, so Ian Hamilton was agan chosen to take the spot kick against stand-in keeper, centre-half Jon Brown, and he coolly scored the winner. Not only did the win serve to revitalise Albion's by now flagging season – it was the first time in more than twenty years that an Albion side had overhauled a two goal deficit away from home.

Another goal against Stoke, this time the equaliser at The Hawthorns

There were still some setbacks to come though – and Stoke City were at the heart of two of them. A week later, the best gate of the season at The Hawthorns – nearly 30,000 – saw runaway leaders Stoke grab a controversial 2-1 win. Bob scored Albion's equaliser that afternoon, and a few weeks later, he scored his fourth goal of the season against the Potters, in the Autoglass Cup tie at the Victoria Ground. A competition record gate (outside the Final) of over 17,000 saw Albion take the lead, when Bob scrambled the ball over the line from close range. They held out until ten minutes from time, when Mark Stein equalised, and in the last minute, with extra time and penalties looming, Stein scored a spectacular winner. "Stoke always seemed to have the voodoo sign over us. I don't think I was ever on the winning side against them. But we'd always give them a game, no thrashings. There was usually only one goal in it – and it was usually Mark Stein who scored it!" Although Bob would go on to play against Stoke many more times in his Albion career, he would, remarkably, never once finish on the winning side against the Potters.

Bob continued to knock in the goals, as Albion, realistically, set their sights more for the Play-offs than automatic promotion. In the second minute of the game against Fulham, David Speedie – another new partner for Bob, on loan from Southampton – won a penalty, and Bob scored his hundredth League goal of his career from the spot. He also scored Albion's consolation goals in defeat at Blackpool and Stockport – although there wasn't much consolation in the

Bob's in there, somewhere; a typical striker's goal in the Autoglass Trophy at Stoke

latter game. Bob had put Albion ahead against their Play-off rivals, at Edgeley Park, only for County to storm back and win 5-1, with their fifth goal being scored by the reviled Paul Williams, who had been sold back to County by Ardiles a few weeks earlier.

When that defeat was followed by another, seven days later, against another challenging side, Port Vale, who thus completed a League 'Double' over the Baggies, things were looking grim again.

Taylor scored more vital goals, against Burnley, in a 2-0 win, and Preston, who were beaten 3-2, to reach 27 for the season, but it was clear that he was carrying too much of the side's scoring burden. 'Stop Bob Taylor, and you stop West Brom,' was the maxim amongst Second Division defenders. True, not many of them succeeded in stopping Bob that season, but he needed someone else to carry the weight.

David Speedie had returned to Southampton after scoring just two goals, and Simon Garner had collected a niggling injury that was keeping him out of the side, and it was clear that Ardiles needed to step into the transfer market. With the Albion seriously short of funds, as usual, he went back to his old club, Newcastle, and signed one of the First Division side's reserve strikers, Andy Hunt, who he had introduced to League football, from Kettering, in his spell at St James' Park.

When Hunt made his full debut for the Albion, at home to Brighton, on April 3, he was clearly lacking in match fitness, not having played in the Newcastle first team all season. He certainly

It's not all glamour; Bob on his backside in the snow at Port Vale, as Donovan breaks away

did not seem to be the answer to Albion's striking problems. When Ardiles signalled that he was to make a substitution in the 63rd minute, with Albion a goal down and looking likely to slip out of a Play-off position for the first time, it was quite a surprise that, instead of taking off the labouring Hunt, he took off Mickey Mellon instead. On came Simon Garner and, between them, he and Hunt turned the game. With Garner running the Brighton defence ragged, Hunt, incredibly, scored an eight minute hat-trick – becoming only the third player in the club's history to do so on his debut.

If the wins over Bolton and Exeter had been vital, it was this remarkable turnaround that really made the season. Taylor and Hunt set up an immediate rapport; not only did that help take the pressure off Bob, it also saw Albion cruise into the Play-offs. Remarkably, Hunt scored nine goals in his ten League games that season. Even more remarkably, and less heralded, Bob scored ten goals, as Albion won seven, drew two and lost just one. "Once Andy Hunt arrived, our results improved dramatically again – when you've got two strikers who're both scoring goals, it's very difficult for opposing defences."

Fittingly, it fell to Taylor to score the goal that effectively booked Albion's Play-off place; the opening goal in a tense match against close rivals Reading. The home side later equalised, but the point was enough to ensure a top six finish for the Baggies, and make Reading wait another year. "I just couldn't stop scoring goals, and we were flying. It was just like the season at Bristol three years

The Taylor goal which clinched Albion's place in the Play-offs, at Elm Park

earlier. Possibly Albion were a better side. We had Darren Bradley sitting there in the middle, and although he had a dodgy knee, he could spray the ball about. At Bristol we had Dave Rennie doing that, with Gary Shelton, who was a strong fit lad, doing all the running about, which Ian Hamilton and Bernard McNally did at the Albion. I wouldn't like to say which side was better, because at Bristol we did the job, and went up automatically, whereas we had to do it the hard way at the Albion, through the Play-offs."

The season ended party-style. In the penultimate game, at Rotherham, late goals from Taylor and Raven supplied a suitable finish for the Albion fans' Beachwear Party, and a week later over 20,000 turned up at The Hawthorns to see what would prove to be Bob's last goal of a momentous season, as Albion relegated poor Hull City, with another thrilling 3-1 win. The three points had another important benefit; results on that final day meant that the two sides that Albion wanted to avoid – Port Vale and Stockport – would meet in the other Play-off semi-final. Albion were paired against the side that they most wanted to face, Swansea City, who they had comprehensively beaten 3-0 at The Hawthorns only five weeks earlier.

On a very wet and windy Sunday afternoon, Albion travelled to the Vetch Field to meet Swansea in the first leg of the semi-finals. When the Albion players tramped off the pitch at the end of the game they – and the fans – knew that they had been very lucky to get away with such a close result. Too many lacklustre or anony-

Bob's final goal of a fantastic season, at Rotherham, as Albion win 2-0

mous individual performances had handed the game to the Welsh side, who, with luck, could well have gone to The Hawthorns with a four goal lead under their belt.

Only Ian Hamilton – who had already suffered the disappointment of losing in the Play-offs three times in his career – could hold his head up high. Two goals early in the second half set Albion back on their heels, and the home side missed two easy chances to add to the score soon after.

It was only after Ardiles brought on Nicky Reid that there was any steel in the Albion defence and midfield. Then, eighteen minutes from time, Albion had a lucky break. Daryl Burgess, of all people, wandered upfield, and bravely managed to get a foot to a through ball, before being clattered to the ground. The ball rose into the air, and dropped right onto the goal line. There, striker Andy McFarlane, who had scored the first goal, and who had caused an enormous amount of trouble with his pace, stood transfixed, as he watched the ball drop. It landed right onto his chest, as he faced his own goal, and bounced into the net.

It was just the life-line that the Albion needed, and they managed to complete the game against a subdued home side, without conceding again. "It was cold, tipping it down, a full house at the Vetch. They overpowered us, they were tough in the tackle and we just didn't seem to know how to handle it. They scored two goals, and we were just grateful to Daryl." There was still the second leg to come, three days later. "Swansea had the edge today, but let's see

Bob can only watch as Daryl Burgess sets up Albion's vital away goal at Swansea

what happens on Wednesday night," declared a relieved Ardiles afterwards. It was the end of Burgess' season; the injury he collected in making that vital goal meant that he would miss the trip to Wembley.

Wednesday April 19 was a day that will never be forgotten by the Albion players who took part. Even now, many of those players, long gone from The Hawthorns, recall that the day was the most special of their careers, and the atmosphere at the game is spoken of in reverential terms by the supporters who were there that night, More than 26,000 crammed into the ground, and created a wall of sound that clearly stimulated the home players – and intimidated the Swansea men.

The game started with a series of crunching tackles from the Albion defence and midfield that set the tone for the game. Albion needed an early goal to level the aggregate, and it came in the seventh minute, with Taylor the provider. He picked up a loose ball, and ran down the left, before crossing perfectly for Andy Hunt to open the scoring from close range. Not only were Albion level on aggregate; if they could only keep Swansea out, they would go through on away goals.

Eight minutes later, Bob was in a similar position, but this time elected to shoot, Roger Freestone pushing the ball out for a corner. Kevin Donovan took it, pushed it to Hamilton, and the midfielder cut along the bye-line before finishing with a surprise shot from an acute angle. With the ground shaking from Albion fans doing their new 'Boing, boing' bounce on the terraces, in a welter of emotion and noise, Albion dominated the game, and missed several clear cut chances to make the tie safe. Catastrophe struck in the 63rd minute, when Mickey Mellon was sent off for foolishly 'studding' Russell Coughlin off the ball. Things got worse moments later when Albion were reduced to nine men for almost five minutes, when Paul Raven had to go off for stitches in a head wound. Swansea got their second wind at that point, and Andy McFarlane missed two golden chances to level the aggregate score.

But this was to be Albion's season, and just when Swansea were getting well on top, a name from Albion's past came back to help. In the 63rd minute, Colin West, who Ardiles had sold to Swansea, came on as a substitute. He had only been on the pitch for eight minutes when he stamped on Ian Hamilton, right in front of the referee. He also received a red card, and with him went Swansea's chances of a Wembley Final. Indeed, Albion created three great chances to wrap up the game after that, missed by Hunt, Bradley and Taylor.

Never mind; after four fraught minutes of injury time, the ground erupted, an ecstatic crowd invaded the pitch and Bob Taylor was chaired off the pitch. He had failed to score in either Play-off game, but the Albion fans knew that SuperBob was responsible for their forthcoming trip to Wembley!

For many years, that game was the high point of Bob's career; but recent events have changed that. "The atmosphere was incredible, but I can't say any longer that it was the biggest thing of my career. I can't get away from the Crystal Palace game in 2002, because that was the biggest thing that has ever happened in my career, getting to the Premiership. But the Swansea game, you just had to be there; people said they could feel the Brummie Road bouncing when they started boinging up and down. Look at my face on the video when we score – I'm just like a banshee, right out of it, because I was so wound up for that game."

After 'scoring for fun' all season, Bob's goals dried up for the three most important games of the season. "I played in every game that season. Ossie wanted to rest me for the little cups, and that, but I wanted to keep on playing and scoring goals. I wanted to get forty goals, and end up the top scorer in Albion's history, which would have been great. But I didn't score in any of the three Play-off games, which was a big disappointment to me."

The Play-off Final was easily the biggest game of Bob's career – up there with the Play-off Final he had played for Leeds against Charlton. It was not the first time he had played at Wembley, he was still very nervous. "I was completely overawed at Wembley, because it was the first proper game I'd ever played there. I'd played there in a reduced time game in the Centenary Trophy for Leeds against Nottingham Forest – but this was the first time properly. Ossie had seen it all before, at Wembley. As soon as we got there, he insisted that everybody have a new suit, ties, and everything. We tried to wangle a pair of shoes out of them as well…but no luck!"

Albion's opponents at Wembley on May 30 were Port Vale, who, eight days earlier, had beaten Stockport County 2-1 at the Empire Stadium in the Autoglass Final. They had only just missed out on automatic promotion, having cruelly been pipped by a dramatic late run by Bolton Wanderers, but were confident that they could beat the Albion, having already beaten them home and away in the League, to finish seven points above them in the table.

If the support of the respective fans meant anything, though, Albion were clear favourites; three quarters of the 54,000 crowd at Wembley wore the blue and white (or green and yellow) of the Baggies. It was

hard to find a Port Vale supporter in the riot of colour in the stands.

It was the first visit of an Albion side to Wembley for more than 23 years; it would also be the last, at least under the famous twin towers. Ardiles selected the same side that had beaten Swansea, but pulled off a surprise by naming Bob's best mate, Gary Robson, as one of the substitutes. In a nervous, edgy game, Albion created the better chances, Kevin Donovan wasting two early opportunities as the first half finished goalless. Five minutes into the second half Albion were denied a clear penalty, when Neil Aspin handled a Taylor header in the area, and soon after Donovan completed a hat-trick of misses when he shot straight at Paul Musselwhite after Bob had put him through.

In the 59th minute came the controversial incident which changed the course of the game. "The referee was Roger Milford, who I knew well because he was a Bristol referee. A great lad, good referee, sensible towards swearing – he'd swear back at you, give you the banter back. Just so long as you didn't cross that line, and disrespect him, and always had time for a laugh and a joke." He had also been the referee at the same stadium on FA Cup Final day 1991, when he had been criticised for his leniency in not sending off Paul Gascoigne in Spurs' win over Nottingham Forest.

This time the official had an easier decision to make – or so it seemed to the 42,000 bellowing Albion fans. Ian Hamilton played a great ball over the top of the Vale defence, and Bob ran on for goal. His former Leeds United team mate, Peter Swan, came in behind him, on the edge of the box, and chopped him down. "Did I play for it? Play for what? The linesman gave the foul, not the referee; that's what I stand by. He's brought me down. I had my body between him and the ball. Swanny made a genuine attempt to go for the ball, but he's brought me down, I'm last man, in front of him, so he's off. If I could have kept my feet, I would have preferred it, because I was right in on goal, and fancied myself to score, ten or fifteen yards out. He took me knee-high, and I went down. And it wasn't Roger who gave it, because he went over to the linesman, he used an extra pair of eyes, and sent Swanny off. I went looking for Peter after the game, and apologized. 'Don't worry about it – it's one of those things.' He was very good about it all."

Swan became only the seventh player to be sent off in seventy years of Wembley history. Albion failed to score from the free kick, but, on the wide open spaces of Wembley, capitalised against Vale's ten men. Ten minutes later, Andy Hunt opened the scoring with a great header after Gary Strodder had hit the post.

Seven minutes from time, *Man of the Match* Nicky Reid scored the only goal of his Albion career to seal the win, and in the last minute, Kevin Donovan added the icing on the cake. "I was involved in the third goal. Nicky Reid crossed from the right, I went for a header with Neil Aspin, and we went down together in a heap. I was trying to dig the ball out and it went for Kevin Donovan, three yards out, and he buried it. He ran straight in front of a photographer, on one knee with his fist up, going 'Yes!!!' It was really dramatic, and the perfect picture. And the cameraman (little Kevin Grice) had just run out of film…"

After two seasons at a level that Albion fans had never thought their club would descend to, they had made a triumphant return to the First Division. Bob's magnificent haul of 37 goals was a new post-War club record, beating the efforts of Albion Superstars such as Jeff Astle, Tony Brown, Derek Kevan, Dave Walsh, Ronnie Allen and Johnny Nicholls; only the great Billy 'Ginger' Richardson had scored more in a season, netting 39 times in 1935-36. What a shame that Ardiles would not be at the helm at the start of the following season.

The Wembley winners against Port Vale. Left to right, back row: Reid, Raven, Bob, Lilwall, Lange, Bradley, Hamilton, Strodder, kitman Dave Matthews, Barry Wylde
Front: Ardiles, McNally, Donovan, Hunt, Garner and Gary Robson

Ming the Merciless

Not long after the Play-off Final, Ossie dropped his bombshell; he was leaving for Tottenham. The Albion board were livid, and Summers threatened to 'send his exocets to White Hart Lane' – but all to no avail. Ossie was gone, Albion collected just £25,000 in compensation, and Keith Burkinshaw was in sole control. "When Keith and Ossie were together, it was like chalk and cheese – a real case of opposites. Ossie was all lively, enthusiastic, upwardly-mobile; Keith was your classic dour 'flat-capped Yorkshireman.' That's the way it came across. He always seemed to be the one that kept Ossie's feet on the ground; that's how it seemed anyway, but when Keith was there on his own, it was never as good. He'd perhaps had his day, when he was with Tottenham, and he was never as good again, at the Albion. I got on well with Keith; I had a bit of banter with him, and I tried to enjoy training with him, but it just didn't work out for him.

Bob had his own theories about why Burkinshaw failed. "He was commuting a lot, because he had his house down south, and he did a lot of travelling. And how could anybody fill Ossie's boots, after the successful season we had just had, and the style of football that we'd played? Comparisons were always going to be made between the two men. All the players loved coming into training under Ossie, and then when he left, you came back to the old routine, and it got a bit monotonous, one thing after another. I think the fans knew that as well, and they got a bit disillusioned with the football."

The new boss may having been lacking in humour, but the players still had their fun. "Keith was known as 'Ming the Merciless' — from Dan Dare. He was a hairy person, and he had this really hairy hand, and you'd be in the dressing room when suddenly, this hairy hand – just like a spider – would flap onto your shoulder, and you'd hear 'Son!' 'Eargh!' It was usually the time when it meant that you were going to be dropped. But that was typical of the sort of banter that the lads were up for, just to try and cheer themselves up under Keith…"

With Albion back in the First Division, great things were expected from all the players – but Bob in particular. If he could score 37 in the Second Division, how many was he likely to score at the higher level? Not many, judging by the way he started in pre-season. Bob played in all five warm-up games, and, like many of the side, looked jaded and out-of-sorts. He failed to score against non-League Enfield, Reading, Kidderminster, West Ham and Chelsea – even though Albion managed to beat both Premiership sides.

Albion's first League match – and their first game at that level for two years — under Keith Burkinshaw was at Oakwell. It was an inauspicious start; the team coach broke down outside Lichfield, the team's pattern broke down after five minutes against Barnsley, with their new player-manager, Viv Anderson, getting off to a scoring debut. With Bob having a stinker, it took a last minute equaliser – after Simon Garner had been sent off – from Kevin Donovan to grab Albion a point.

Four days later, Bob was back in Bristol, as Albion won 4-1 at Twerton Park in the first leg of the Coca Cola Cup. Once again he failed to get off the mark, but had two goals disallowed, one, a diving header, for offside, the other because the referee decided to award Albion a free kick instead of applying the advantage rule.

Things got even worse in the second leg, Bob missing a penalty for the first time when he struck the crossbar, in a goalless draw at The Hawthorns. At this point, whilst always being supportive of Bob, the fans were talking about him in the same breath as banjos and cow's backsides... The next game, at Stoke, was lost to a solitary goal from – inevitably – Mark Stein, and Albion were already struggling.

It was not until his eleventh outing that Bob finally got amongst the goals. The occasion was Albion's first-ever meeting with Southend United, under The Hawthorns' floodlights, and Bob struck twice early in the second half, and went close to a double-quick hat-trick soon after. The evening was not to have a happy ending, for Brett Angel – who would later play along-side Bob for a spell on loan at the Albion – scored two controversial late goals to grab a point for the Shrimpers.

Despite the disappointing result, it was a great time for Bob to break his duck, for the next match was the much awaited Black Country Derby against the Wolves, live on ITV, and he was raring to go when he reported for duty on the Sunday morning before the game. Unfortunately, he was covered with spots – and had to be sent home immediately, having contracted chicken pox! It was the first game he had missed since signing from Bristol City – and he failed to even see the game on TV, because the broadcast did not reach as far south as Bob's home in Weston. "I'd missed the game against the Wolves when we won 3-2 – because I'd got chicken pox. I was itching like crazy, sitting in my boxer shorts in the living room, with headphones on, listening to the game on the radio."

The game was a real cracker, won 3-2 for Albion with a tremendous 25 yarder from Bradley, and a diving header by Donovan. Bob missed two games, reappearing, bearded, and a stone lighter after his illness, as a second half substitute in an Anglo-Italian qualifying game against Peterborough. On September 18 Bob scored the one hundredth goal of his League career (with Leeds, Bristol and Albion) to give Albion a half time lead at home to Crystal Palace, but Albion capitulated in the second half to lose 4-1. Once he had started scoring, Bob soon got back to his old form. He scored in successive games against Middlesbrough, Derby (a classic 5-3 defeat at the Baseball Ground, his fiftieth goal for the club) and Chelsea, as Albion went out of the Coca Cola Cup at Stamford Bridge.

Four days after that cup exit, Albion made a quick return to London, and a first ever visit to Millwall's New Den. Bob failed to make it four in a row; in fact, it was Bob who needlessly brought down Alex Rae in the box to concede the penalty which settled the game…

It was nine goals in nine games after Bob's next two outings, when he scored Albion's only goal in a 2-1 home defeat by Pescara in the Anglo-Italian, and two more in a 3-0 win against a wretched Peterborough side. Bob was even being compared with Germany's great goalscorer, Gerd Muller, when he scored again, in a 4-1 win over Watford. He scored again on November 6, this time against his 'favourite' opposition, Bolton Wanderers. This time it was from the penalty spot, after he had been brought down by Aiden Davison; the Bolton keeper was sent off, which meant that the first touch for the Trotters' new on-loan keeper, was to pick the ball out of the back of the net after facing Bob's spot kick. The name of that young keeper? Russell Hoult! There was no happy ending this time; Bolton's ten men fought back brilliantly in the second half, and for the second time Albion threw away a two goal lead.

The season hit rock bottom seven days later, with a dreadful 2-1 FA Cup defeat at non-League Halifax – the second time that Albion had been humbled by non-League opposition in the space of four seasons. "They were Conference at the time, and we got beat 2-1 – but the best thing about that was that we had all of our gear on the bus, and we went straight from The

Another classic volley by Bob, in the 4-1 win over Portsmouth at The Hawthorns

Shay, right to the airport, and jetted out to Italy, for the Anglo-Italian Cup. We just got on the bus and got away to go to Fiorentina. So we didn't face the wrath of the fans and the press, which was something, at least."

Gradually – despite Bob's goals – Albion were slipping down the table, mostly because of their poor away record. Indeed, it was not until a 3-0 win at Southend on December 6 that Albion won away from The Hawthorns. Both Taylor and Hunt scored in that game, to bring their totals up to a dozen goals each – the first time that Albion had had two strikers both in double figures before Christmas since Tony Brown and Jeff Astle had hit 35 between them by Christmas 1965.

Eleven days later, Bob scored his second goal in the Anglo-Italian Cup – in front of the smallest attendance ever to witness a Bob Taylor goal, as just 47 paying customers turned up for a meaningless fixture in Cosenza, three days before Christmas.

Domestic form really slumped in the new year, when a run of defeats – culminating in a real shocker at Peterborough – saw Albion slip into the bottom four for the first time. The Hunt-Taylor partnership had been broken up because of the former Newcastle man's leg injury, and Keith Burkinshaw brought in young Graham Fenton on loan from Aston Villa. On February 5 the youngster scored a great goal to give Albion their first win in eleven games, before returning to the Villa.

Three weeks later, Albion took on rivals Wolves at

Bob is just about to go belly up at Molineux, after scoring the equaliser

Molineux. They were expected to lose – they were expected to get thrashed, by Wolves fans, at least – pulled they pulled off a remarkable win. Bob scored Albion's equaliser, then risked life and limb… "Bernie went for the tackle and the ball ricocheted out to me – I don't think he actually passed it to me. I took it on and slotted it past the keeper's left. Our fans were behind the goal, and I went to do a handstand to celebrate, but I think it had been raining, and as I put my hands down, I slipped, and all my weight went on my right hand. Fortunately, as I slipped, I rolled as well, so all my weight went onto my shoulder, otherwise I think I'd have broken my neck that day. I still laugh at that when I see it on the video…" Paul Mardon, Bob's former Bristol City colleague, chose a great day to score his first-ever League goal, to head a great winning goal.

That win took Albion back up as high as 18th, but defeats against Palace, Derby and Middlesbrough meant a quick return to the relegation zone. The crucial game came on Wednesday April 27, a rearranged home fixture against fellow-strugglers Birmingham City. It was a game that Albion dare not lose, for they would surely be sucked into a last day relegation drama. They lost. They dominated the first half against Barry Fry's men, and Kevin Donovan gave them the lead, only for Steve Claridge, Louis Donowa and Andy Saville to give Blues a 3-1 lead early in the second half. Daryl Burgess – scoring the last goal in front of the soon-to-be demolished Brummie Road terraces – gave Albion hope, only for Claridge to score Blues' fourth two minutes from time. Now it really was crisis time. Three days later they beat Grimsby at The Hawthorns – defeat in that one would have meant certain doom — leaving themselves with two tough away games to finish the season.

The first came in midweek, at Kenilworth Road, in which two ordinary sides produced a quite extraordinary game – a triumph of incident against football quality.

What made the game more intriguing was that the future of both clubs was at stake; each required a win for absolute safety. Albion had just recorded a win against Grimsby, whilst Luton had at least ended a 600 minute barren spell with goals in their games against Southend and Millwall, yet still they had not won for nine games.

There was controversy from the start; the Kenilworth Road pitch was an absolute quagmire, which was remarkable, because it hadn't rained for days; the Luton groundstaff had been watering it for hours before the kick-off, to make it more amenable to the home side's long ball game, prompting Albion to make an official (but fruitless, because, technically, they hadn't broken any rules) protest to the League.

The first half was dreadful, from Albion's point of view, as Keith Burkinshaw decided to defend for the draw which would definitely put his side above Oxford and might be enough to overhaul Blues. They ceded complete possession to Luton, who won eleven corners to Albion's none, and were very fortunate to concede just one goal, to Preece, in the 35th minute.

Ten minutes into the second half, SuperBob stepped up to play his part, when he scored what will go down as the outstanding goals of his career; one totally out of context with the game so far. "That was when I scored the best dribbled goal I've ever scored. As I said at the time, 'I haven't dribbled like that since I was a baby!" Later Kevin Donovan did an identical dribble, but hit the post, and Lee Ashcroft scored. But Kevin's was much better than mine – because he knew what he was doing! I didn't have a clue what I was doing. It was on a boggy pitch, and I had the ball at my feet, and you can take defenders on, and they can't twist and turn to follow you. I went past two or three people and ended up in the box, and in it went. I poked it under the keeper. Not my best goal – but different to most of the goals I normally score, headers and little shots. It really surprised me, and I couldn't believe it."

Eight minutes later, Daryl Burgess and the Luton keeper, Sommer clashed heads, which led to both of them being stretchered off and taken to hospital. Mickey Mellon replaced Burgess, with Ian Hamilton dropping to right back, and Neil Parsley moving into the centre; Sommer was replaced by a young keeper, Andy Petterson (who would one day join the Albion on loan), who looked rather unsound. Incredibly, just thirty seconds later, it was Stuart Naylor's turn; the Albion keeper took a knock on the head as he raced out of his area to clear, and was helped, staggering, off the field, with a broken cheekbone. It was the first time in the history of the Football League that both substitute keepers had been used in the same game… Tony Lange came on for his first appearance in nearly three months, but his first touch of the ball was to pick it out of the net after James had headed in from a corner kick that Naylor had conceded with his final touch,

There was an immediate chance for Bob to equalise when Petterson missed a long cross, but in the 76th minute Luton were coasting when John Hartson scored their third. Albion looked dead and buried, but two minutes after Luton's third goal, Kevin Donovan went on another amazing long dribble that was possibly better that Bob's – in that he beat four defenders with pure skill – but spoiled it all by miskicking his shot onto the post. Fortunately, Lee Ashcroft was on hand to scramble the ball over the line, to make it 3-2, with everything to play for in the last twelve minutes.

In the end, Albion just could not summon up enough reserves of strength to score a third; in fact, Luton went close to a fourth, when Lange had to make a brilliant save from Michael Oakes' shot. In the last minute, the game descended into farce when Mitchell Thomas and Gary Strodder (who had been pushed up front as an emergency striker) started scrapping, and the referee had no alternative but to send both men off.

The Luton game set the scene quite starkly for the following Sunday. Before the final series of games, Albion were out of the bottom three – Oxford United and Peterborough were already down – only on goal difference. Both they and Birmingham City had 48 points from 45 games, but Albion were eight goals better off on goal difference. That meant that a win, at 15th placed Portsmouth, would, realistically, save Albion at Blues expense. However, should Albion fail to win at Fratton Park – one of their favourite grounds in the past – then Blues could well send them down if they could get a better result against Tranmere Rovers at Prenton Park. Tranmere, like Portsmouth, had little to play for, but for a different reason – they had already qualified for the Play-offs.

Albion had their injury problems for the game. Stuart Naylor, of course, was definitely out with a broken cheekbone, whilst Burgess was out because of the League ruling that any player taken to hospital with concussion must be rested for two weeks. Even so, it meant that Burkinshaw was able to field no less than eight of the side which had been so successful at Wembley twelve months before. In contrast, the thousands of Albion fans who had travelled south to cheer their side – and enjoy another Beachwear Party – must have been heartened when the Portsmouth fans presented their *Player of The Year* trophies before the game – to players who were all unable to play. Warren Neill and Alan McLaughlin emerged from the stand in suits, rather than kit, to collect their medals, and with top scorer Gerry Creaney suspended, and former Albion striker John Durnin also injured, the odds looked very much on Albion's side. "I can remember the build-up to the game very well, when we had about 10,000 in the ground, and thousands more outside. The approaches to Portsmouth are very narrow, with those little streets, and I remember that we couldn't get any closer than about five hundred yards in the coach, because the streets were full of Baggies fans. You just couldn't move, so we all had to get out the coach and walk through the fans. It was like being at a mass riot – nothing was actually kicking off – but we could hardly get through."

And that's the way it proved, although not without some heart-stopping moments. The first such came not from Fratton Park but from Prenton Park, as the news filtered through over the airwaves that Louis Donowa had put Blues ahead against Tranmere. It meant that, with just sixty minutes of the season remaining, Albion were, as things stood, relegated. That changed six minutes before the break. The ever-industrious SuperBob won the ball in midfield, despite loud calls for handball from the home fans, and laid the ball wide to Ian Hamilton. He beat his man for speed and crossed to the far post, where Lee Ashcroft, running in, caught the ball awkwardly, with the side of his face. It still had enough pace to beat the despairing dive of Pompey keeper Alan Knight — although he did get a palm to the ball – and the two defenders on the line. Albion were ahead – they just had to make sure that it stopped that way!

It took a couple of minutes to clear the pitch of celebrating Albion fans, and, as the interval drew close, David Elleray bizarrely blew his whistle a full two minutes early. Albion were in no position to complain about his timekeeping…

If Albion fans had enjoyed the first half, they were not too happy with the second, as Portsmouth came out like a whirlwind. In the 50th minute, with youngster Scott Darton vainly appealing for offside, Chamberlain rolled the ball across the Albion goal, for Paul Hall, rushing in, to fire at goal; somehow both Lange and Parsley threw themselves simultaneously at the ball to scramble it away. Three minutes later came the turning point of the game, when Hall cut in from the wing to fire in a great shot that was heading for the top corner, only for Lange to make the save of the season to tip the ball round the post.

Portsmouth were never quite as dangerous again, and when the news came through that Tranmere had equalised against Blues, Albion knew they had some sort of a cushion from relegation. That could have been illusory, though, as Blues scored a last minute winner at Tranmere, which meant that a Portsmouth equaliser would have relegated the Baggies – who had McNally and Strodder to thank for clearing late shots from Wood and Chamberlain off the line. As a result of the late start of the second half at Portsmouth – because of crowd trouble during the interval – Albion had to battle for another six minutes after the final score at Tranmere, before they knew they were safe. Cue wild celebrations from Albion fans – which carried on to the following day, when thousands broke down the gates of the soon to be demolished Birmingham Road End to gain illegal entry to the Gary Robson Testimonial. It's not often you see a sell-out crowd for a testimonial game, but Albion fans were on a real high after their narrow escape.

"It's just a blur now, but it was a great day at Portsmouth, and we got the result, and the joy and the celebrations afterwards. And we celebrated as well – we had the beers on the bus. It was the old double-decker, and I ended up in the 'boot section' of the coach, enjoying a few cans!"

It had been a mixed season for Bob. He was pleased, of course, that the club had avoided instant relegation, and he was certainly happy with his haul of twenty goals from the season, considering his early season problems with illness and injury. There was plenty to look forward to in 1994-95 – although, as it would turn out, not entirely under the management of Keith Burkinshaw.

The Alan Buckley era

There were hopes of an improvement in Albion's fortunes in 1994, following the club's radical new share issue. Not that the move brought in a huge sum of money; certainly not enough to speculate in the transfer market. As a result, Albion's only major signing during the summer was former Norwich City and Manchester United midfielder, Mike Phelan, and it was obvious that that would not be enough to prevent a repeat of the previous season's problems.

Bob played in all of the pre-season friendlies, which started off with wins at Halesowen, Yeovil and Kidderminster Harriers. Bob's first goals of the season came on August 2, the first two goals in a comfortable 3-0 win against Swansea at the Vetch Field. Four days later, Albion made a stunning comeback at Ninian Park, scoring three goals in the last five minutes to win a game that they had been losing 2-0. It was Bob who scored the last two Albion goals, and he certainly looked sharp for the new campaign, which kicked off in earnest at Kenilworth Road on Saturday August 13. So sharp, in fact, that he scored the second fastest League goal of the season – second to his former colleague, Simon Garner, at Wycombe – in the fourth minute of the game against Luton. It was also Albion's fastest opening to a season since Ally Brown had scored against Ipswich after just 39 seconds in 1978.

However, without the injured Andy Hunt up front alongside Bob, Albion looked a poor side, and in the end they were grateful for a point. Three days later, there was an embarrassing goalless draw against Hereford United (then in Division Three) at Edgar Street in the first leg of the Coca Cola Cup. The home side were poor, but Albion were worse, failing to get a goal against a side reduced to ten men by the 35th minute dismissal of Tim Steele. Albion only created one real chance, which fell to Bob, in the 62nd minute, but he could only slam Donovan's shot against the underside of the crossbar.

Two more away games followed – as the result of Albion's rebuilding of the Birmingham Road End. The first was a disaster – a spineless 2-0 defeat against the old enemy at Molineux – the second little better, a goalless draw at Swindon. And there was worse to come when The Hawthorns was open again for business for the visit of Hereford, as Albion tumbled out of the cup on the end of a shock 1-0 defeat. Bob missed the game, because he had to go to hospital for tests following the presence of blood in his urine, but he was back three days later for the trip to The New Den. He had a new strike partner; with Hunt still out, and no money being made available by the board, Burkinshaw had signed Dutch striker Jeroen Boere on loan from West Ham.

The two strikers seemed to click immediately, although it was Bob who scored both goals in a 2-2 draw. That result meant that by mid-September, Albion were bottom of the table, without a win in eight games, but the first win of the season came on September 24 when Bob headed the only goal of the game to give Albion what was perhaps an undeserved victory against Burnley at The Hawthorns.

Bob's scoring record at the Albion was generating a considerable amount of interest amongst other clubs, particularly as it was obvious that Albion, as always, were short of cash. Manchester City were the first club to express an interest, but it was Coventry who actually started the bidding. Aware of Albion's continuing interest in full-back Paul Williams (who had earlier been on loan at the Albion) Coventry offered £500,000 in cash plus Paul Williams and John Williams. That was increased to £1.25m plus Paul Williams and Mike Quinn, and then, as a final offer, when Burkinshaw made it clear that he was not interested in Quinn, the Sky Blues increased their bid to £1.5m plus Paul Williams.

Chairman Trevor Summers, wary of Bob's popularity with the fans, and with his own position in jeopardy, turned the offers down flat. He was hoping to raise cash for players with a new share offer, not by selling the club's greatest asset – but the question of Bob's future at the Albion was a topic that would linger for the rest of the season. Not that it would worry Keith Burkinshaw for much longer. After three consecutive defeats, and with the club in freefall, he was dismissed.

The writing was on the wall for the match against Tranmere at Prenton Park on Saturday October 15. By then, an unholy alliance of Tony Hale and Graham Waldron, Albion's chief shareholders, had forced Trevor Summers to step down as chairman, in favour of Hale. At Tranmere, in a bizarre leaving gesture, Summers decided to cross a line that had never been crossed by an Albion chairman before – he sat on the players' bench throughout the game. Most of the team were unaware of Summer's faux pas until the game was well underway – but none of them were too happy about it. Youngster Carl Heggs was enraged, even if he had difficulty in explaining his ire. "I was so angry with Trevor Summers being on the bench. You've got to watch what you say, but I nearly called him a pineapple!" Bob was more sanguine at the time. "It was quite a shock, but I just had a bit of a giggle. It wasn't very professional; he never came down before the game to see the players and wish them all the best, so why should he come down on the bench and start shouting at them?"

On October 4, Hale had given Burkinshaw the dreaded 'vote of confidence,' whilst warning "Managers have a sixth sense about these things, like wounded elephants going to their graves to die" – and demanding that his manager sack his number two, Dennis Mortimer, and appoint John Trewick. Burkinshaw, not surprisingly, did nothing of the sort, although Mortimer — Aston Villa through and through — was not popular with either the players or the supporters.

The day after Albion lost 3-1 at Tranmere, Burkinshaw stormed on the subject of the director on the bench, "I had better not say anything – except that it will not happen again." Not with Burkinshaw as manager, at any rate; the following day he was sacked – but not before, disgracefully, the news was deliberately leaked to the *Evening Mail*, with the result that Mortimer read about his sacking in the press before the club informed him personally. Burkinshaw's last comment was a telling one. "Unless serious money comes into the club, Albion will never do anything unless they are fantastically lucky."

John Trewick took over as caretaker manager, and guided the side to a vital home win over Sheffield United. The new boss – Bob's fourth at the Albion in just two and a half years – was watching that match from the stand, and on Thursday October 20 Alan Buckley was appointed on a three and a half year contract.

Buckley did not get off to a good start, although he was warmly welcomed at the start of his first game, at Barnsley. "When I heard that reception from the travelling fans, I had to look round, because I thought SuperBob must have come out behind me," said Buckley, who had very quickly picked up on just how popular Bob Taylor was with the fans.

Buckley was also very quick to explain his position over Bob's possible departure to *The Baggies* newspaper, who had devoted a special issue to the possibility of Taylor's departure. "I know Bob's contract is up this season. If he leaves, it will be his decision – not mine and not the board's. And you can tell that to every Albion fan. If Bob Taylor goes, don't blame me, or the directors, because we all want Bob to stay, because he's a brilliant player. It's all down to Bob."

Bob replied in *The Baggies*. "Football is all about ambition. Yes, I'd love to play in the Premier League, and win medals, but I also like playing football here. I've settled here, and it's great. At the end of the day, whether I stay at the Albion, it ain't up to me. It's down to the people upstairs and whether they have the ambition for the club to reach the top. I'm 27 now, and I've got to look after my future."

Bob always got on well with Alan Buckley. "He had his temper, and all, but he was really down to earth with it – not like some managers I could mention! He'd give it to you straight, and he was always in the dressing room, and you could have a bit of banter with him. He'd come in for a cup of tea and have a bit of a dig at you. He loved his five a sides at the old GKN gym, and he still had a good touch, and he was a great finisher as well. Very passionate about the game. We did try to play football under him, and we enjoyed it. He had a good assistant manager, the late Arthur Mann, who was a great lad. We nicknamed him Jean Luc – Jean Luc Picard, for obvious reasons!"

But those famous Buckley tantrums... "There was the other side to Alan – his tantrums, when the plastic cups would go. In fact, I think that's why we had plastic cups in the dressing room! Once he'd got it out of him, it was forgotten; he never held a grudge against anybody. The aggression was channeled in the right direction, I think. He was passionate about something, but once he'd blown his top, it was all over. I remember once at Luton, away. We got beat and Alan came in at the end, into this tiny dress-

The perils of the game; Bob is stretchered off (nothing too serious!) at The Valley

70

ing room, when Paul Mitchell, the physio, was bending down, looking at someone who had twisted his ankle. We just heard this ranting and raving coming up the tunnel, and then, just like a cowboy film, the door was booted open, swinging inwards, and the corner of the door hit Paul right between the eyes. It opened up immediately, blood everywhere, stitches and everything. To be honest, it killed it a bit for us. We were going to get a real bollocking, but after that it was all, 'Sorry Mitch' and it calmed things down. It took the edge off it – we still got a bollocking, but it was nowhere near as bad as it was going to be. When it happened, you just wanted to laugh, but you couldn't, because you knew what you were going to get!"

It was not until Buckley's fifth game in charge that Taylor got off the mark with his sixth goal of the season – a volleyed equaliser against Charlton at The Valley – but he followed that up six days later with the third goal, a classic header, in a 3-2 home win against Oldham. Sadly, with interest in him by other clubs at its height, and Albion struggling, particularly away from home, Bob would not score again for another three months – his worst goal drought to date.

And there was worse to come, for at Roots Hall, on December 27 1994, Bob was sent off for the first time in his Albion career (he had been sent off once before, for Bristol City, against Bolton). Seven minutes from time, with Albion losing 2-1 to Southend, despite having dominated the game, Bob saw red. "I think I was hard done by. The first yellow card was for mouthing, because I complained when somebody did me from behind – but that was fair game, I suppose. But the second one, we just went in for a tackle, came out of it, and the referee. Mr Pierce, reckoned it was a foul, booked me, and I was off." It earned Bob a one match ban, against Reading – where, fortuitously, Albion recorded their much delayed first away win of the season.

Bob would have missed the Reading game anyway – as he missed the FA Cup ties with Coventry City – because of the recurrence of a hamstring injury that kept him out of the side for three weeks. He returned to the side for the prestigious friendly against Swedish champions IFK Gothenberg, scoring one of the goals in a 4-1 shock win against the Champions League qualifiers, but would struggle with his form for the rest of the season. For once he was no longer first choice for the number nine shirt. Alan Buckley had bought in former Welsh international and Grimsby striker Tony Rees — "An unusual sort of striker, very keen of backheels!" —

and the two men would alternate between first choice striker and the substitute's bench.

It was Bob who was given the nod for the home game against Stoke City on February 25, as Albion slumped to a 3-2 defeat; Bob ended the game with his arm in a sling after a bad knock – but at least that meant he was able to miss out on the ultimate indignity, as Buckley ordered the entire first team to turn out in the Central League game against Everton Reserves at Goodison Park, three days after the Stoke match. As well as that 1-1 draw, Bob also missed the 'six-pointer' against Burnley at Turf Moor, which ended with a similar scoreline, and saw the Albion drop to 19th place in Division One.

The next game, against fellow strugglers Portsmouth, on March 8, was a key one for the Baggies. The home side, although struggling somewhat in the table, had not lost at Fratton Park in 1995 and Albion, with only one win in their last ten games, were not expected to dent that record. That was to bargain without Super-Bob – even though he was only drafted into the starting line-up because Tony Rees failed a late fitness test.

There was a theory going around the fans in West Bromwich that if only Bob could get a goal, no matter how lucky – 'off his backside' or whatever – then the goals would flow once again. And that's what happened at Fratton Park, scene of Albion's last day survival in 1994.

Bob's on the deck, but the ball's in the net against Wolves — a great diving header

72

Gerry Creaney gave Portsmouth a 36th minute lead, and the home side dominated the game, with Albion having Stuart Naylor to thanks for a series of fine saves. Then, two minutes before the break, Bob struck – in comical fashion. He collected a pass from Andy Hunt, ran on a few yards, then let fly from 25 yards. The shot, as so often during the season, was not a good one. It was weak, and veteran goalkeeper Alan Knight had it covered, but, inexplicably, the keeper let the ball go straight through him and into the net.

The goal had the desired effect; Bob was revitalised in the second half, and eight minutes from time he went close to a second goal when he had a shot blocked, the follow-up cleared off the

Bob turns on the style to net in the 5-1 demolition of Tranmere Rovers

line, and a header onto the bar. Five minutes later, with the Albion fans very happy with the draw, he did strike, shooting home from ten yards after a great run by Paul Agnew.

The three points lifted Albion an amazing five places in the table, and did wonders for the team's confidence. Which was just as well, because they faced high-riding Wolves at home, eight days later. Their local rivals were on a real high, and pushing for automatic promotion, when they arrived at The Hawthorns for a midweek game that was featured on *Central TV*. The result was completely unexpected, as Albion triumphed by two goals to nil. The first goal was scored early on, by winger Lee Ashcroft, but the game is remembered more for Bob's contribution.

"Lee Ashcroft had a great game that night. He had Jamie Smith in his pocket all game, and he got him sent off in the end. Lee scored the first goal with a header, early on, and then, early in the second half, he won possession on the halfway line, out on the left, and he beat one player, and outpaced Jamie Smith, and he put over a great cross. I can still see it now; it was like it was in slow motion, because the ball came across and I went in between two defenders, and I dived in between the two. I got my head to it and it went into the bottom corner. I always saw that as one of my favourite goals; partly because it was against the Wolves – but also, Jimmy Greaves said on TV what a great goal it was, and that was good enough for me!"

In the end, that result saw Wolves finish six points short of automatic promotion, and they went out to Bolton in the Play-off semi-finals. Albion won four more games before the end of the season, and Bob managed one more goal – in another excellent 5-1 win over more Play-off candidates, Tranmere. Although they only finished 19th, there was a ten point gap between Albion and the highest-placed relegated side, Swindon.

Bob finished the worst season of his Albion career with just eleven goals, all scored in the League, yet his value in the transfer market had never been higher; at one point he was being valued around two million pounds, and the subject of interest of no less than four Premier League clubs, as well as Sunderland, who were offering cash plus midfielder Shaun Cunnington.

On August 1 1995, Bob agreed to sign the new three year contract that he had been pushing for – and on the same day that Alan Buckley took on Shaun Cunnington on trial from Sunderland; one of a number of former Grimsby men that the manager was to bring to The Hawthorns.

Losing, losing... and losing

Albion played seven pre-season friendlies in July and August 1995. The highlight of the sequence was a home game against Aston Villa on August 1. Unusually for a warm-up game, crowd congestion delayed the start of the game, such was the anticipation of what had become a rare meeting between the two old rivals. Villa included former Albion YTS player Ugo Ehiogu and £9.3m worth of talent in the shape of Mark Draper, Gareth Southgate and Savo Milosovic. Villa fans filled the whole of the Smethwick End, the gate itself was an impressive 16,299, but it was SuperBob who overshadowed Villa's new Yugoslavian striker when he scored the only goal of the game in the 67th minute.

The goal was a sweet one – even sweeter for Albion fans because earlier in the day Bob had pledged his future to the Albion for the next three years. He had been in contractual talks which had finally come to a satisfactory conclusion. His strike against the Villa was the icing on the cake. A misjudgment by Paul McGrath enabled Taylor to race on to Kevin Donovan's through ball, and from a tight angle, clip a precision finish over the keeper's body.

It did not take Bob long to get off the mark in the campaign proper. On the opening day, debutant Dave Gilbert scored Albion's winner against Charlton at The Hawthorns. The following Tuesday Albion were disappointingly held by Third Division Northampton Town, in the Coca-Cola Cup, but Bob was on the mark in the 41st minute, when he glanced home a header from a cross from another new signing, Tony Brien.

Next it was on to Molineux. Bob has always had a penchant for scoring against the Wolves, and this game was no exception. Albion were much the better side in the first half, but Stuart Naylor got injured, requiring four minutes treatment just before the interval. During his dazed spell he could only watch in horror as Bob deflected a Gordon Cowans free kick onto his own post – the nearest Bob would ever come to an own goal against the Albion! A minute after the break, in blazing sunshine, Bob headed in a cross at the right end, from Andy Hunt, to give Albion the lead, only for Paul Mardon to really show him how it was done, with a 66th minute own goal that gifted Wolves a point.

Growing in confidence Albion went to the Sixfields Stadium at Northampton for the first time for the second leg of their Coca Cola Cup tie, and overcame a difficult hurdle with, in the end, an easy 4-2 win. Bob, forging a useful partnership with Andy Hunt, scored two more goals.

It seemed now that, after a summer of unease, Bob had settled down once more. He had been out of contract, and Premier clubs had been sniffing around, but despite expressing interest, neither Coventry nor QPR pursued the matter any further.

After scoring four goals early on, Bob then suffered something of a drought, netting just twice in eleven games in League and Cup. It had not helped that, during that dry spell, Bob had picked up one of his more unusual – and painful — injuries, perforating an eardrum during training before the game against Birmingham City on September 17. Although his balance was affected by the injury, Bob gamely played on but the injury – caused by a whack on the head – did cause him some trouble for a number of weeks.

Whilst Bob was going through his first barren spell, Albion were going out of the Coca Cola Cup; after grabbing a much-deserved 1-1 draw at Elm Park, they were beaten 4-2 by Reading in the second leg of the tie at The Hawthorns. It was the nature of that defeat that caused Alan Buckley to re-evaluate his team's tactics, and as a result, he decided to switch from his more usual 4-4-2 to a 4-5-1 formation, with Bob playing the lone striker's role. The opponents in the next game were, once again, Reading, and Albion won 2-0 to gain a little revenge for their shock cup exit. Bob scored Albion's second goal, sweeping in a cross from Kevin Donovan, and Tony Brown, writing in the *Sports Argus*, was quick to praise Bob's contribution to Albion's new style, both against Reading and, in the next game, against Italian opposition. "Bob Taylor really seems to be revelling in his new role as Albion's lone striker. His performances against Reading, and Foggia were two of his best this season. I feel he is the right man for that arduous task, because he seems to thrive in the extra workload. He is lucky enough to have such good support from midfield players such as Donovan, Cunnington, Ashcroft and Gilbert. The key is Bob's body strength. All you

Bob scores against Port Vale at The Hawthorns in 1995-96

76

can do in that situation is hold the ball up and he does that because he is so hard to knock off the ball."

The Foggia game ended in defeat, but Albion bounced back with wins at Luton and at home to Portsmouth, with Andy Hunt's eighth minute goal sending Albion up as high as second place in the table. The game marked Alan Buckley's first year in charge – a year that had been marked by steady progress – and the win left the club with the possibility of entering a second year at the very top of the table, if they could win against third place Millwall at the New Den and Leicester lost at home to Crystal Palace.

What followed next was extraordinary. From the brink of the leadership of the Second Division, Albion suffered the most stunning run of results in the whole of their long, proud history.

Albion got off to a bad start, when they fell behind to a 19th minute goal, but Andy Hunt equalised two minutes later only for Uwe Fuchs to sweep home a cross from Jason van Blerk to give Millwall the lead once more. Despite sustained pressure, Albion could not find an equaliser, although Bob did miss an easy chance, heading wide from a Hamilton centre. Leicester did lose at home to Crystal Palace and for the third time in a month Albion missed out on the chance to go top. Instead, it was Millwall who went to the top of the table; how they and Albion would suffer from that day on...

Albion had a chance to recover lost ground the following Sunday when they had another top of the table clash in front of the TV cameras at home to Leicester City. The game was over as a contest by the interval, with Albion three goals down to Martin O'Neill's men; Albion did score two goals to make the second half a little more interesting, but, to be frank, that was because City eased up, rather than any battling qualities exhibited by Buckley's men.

Inexplicably, the defeats just kept on coming. Eleven on the trot in the League. It was not that Albion played particularly badly – but, obviously, to say that they were not playing particularly well is an understatement. Everything seemed to go against them in that astonishing run; deflections, poor refereeing decisions, shots against the woodwork – everything conspired to see them lose... and lose... and lose.

"It was just one of those things. You get beat once, twice, three times. Then you start to think that you have to do something about it, and you get beat four, five, six... yet we weren't playing that badly, really, but we weren't getting the rub of the green. Bucko kept changing captains; it was just one of those superstitious things. We got beat, and he'd say, 'Here, you can be the captain.' It was the thirteenth game, and we were playing Wolves, and it was my turn to be captain, and we got the nil-nil to end the run. So I kept the captaincy, and we hardly lost a game after that. We drew a lot, but we hardly lost a game again that season, while I was captain. I kept the armband until the end of the season, I think we lost the one game, at home to Luton; it was great."

With Albion fans hardly able to believe what they were witnessing, the run finally came to an end on January 13 1996, when Albion drew 0-0 in a key game at home to Wolves. Had Albion lost that game, the writing would surely have been on the wall for Alan Buckley – even though, inexplicably, chairman Tony Hale had actually extended his manager's contract in the middle of the losing run, thus dropping a financial millstone around his own neck the next time he might want to sack his manager.

Albion should have won the game, with Andy Hunt missing a penalty, but the following week it was backs to the wall again, as they lost at Charlton (4-1) and, the week after, at Ipswich. Bob scored in the game at Portman Road – his first League goal since before the start of the disastrous run, way back on October 7.

If that had not been embarrassing enough, Albion had also been dumped out of the FA Cup by Second Division opposition, losing 4-3 in their third round tie at Crewe. The closeness of the final scoreline belies the reality – with a young Neil Lennon bossing the midfield, Albion were outclassed by the Alex, and were 4-1 down at one stage, and looking a club record Cup defeat as well.

After that game, the waiting press corps, eager to interview Buckley, were privy to a typical Buckley dressing room 'lock-in.' Buckley kept his players in the dressing room for well over an hour, and the din emanating from the room got louder and louder, culminating in a confrontation between the manager and winger Lee Ashcroft, who squared up to each other.

"You had two hotheads there; Bucko and Ashy — it was frustration. You get somebody shouting at you, and you're already disappointed, and you think you're getting picked on, and your natural defences just come up, and there was a bit of a set-to between the two of them." Even Bob had experienced the Buckley temper. "I had something like it myself with Buckley. We'd just signed a lot of players from Grimsby – I think we had six or seven of them in the side – and we were playing Grimsby at The Hawthorns. He had a real go at me; "Taylor, are you going to get off your arse and start playing?" And I turned round and said, "**** off!" And I went out and I scored, a header from a Sneekes cross. Then a few minutes later I got put through and I lobbed the keeper who came out. We won 3-1. I don't know whether that was a tactical thing by Bucko, to get me riled and worked up – but I did knock on his door the following day, and went in to apologise. In the dressing room, he'd said to me, 'If you ever say that to me again, that'll be it!' The day after he was as nice as pie; 'It's one of those things, son, just forget about it.' He wasn't bothered at all; all part and parcel of the game."

Yet despite the problems in their domestic programme, Albion were actually having some success in the much-derided Anglo-Italian Cup. On November 8 Reggiana had visited The Hawthorns. By now Bob had been relegated to the substitute's bench, but he came on as a replacement for Kevin Donovan, and scored Albion's winner, knocking in an Andy Hunt cross to give ten man Albion – Paul Mardon was sent off near the end – a 2-1 win.

Albion had drawn their first game in the competition, in Salerno, then lost their next, at home to Foggia, and were expected, once more, to make an early exit, with a tough final game to come in Italy, in Brescia. The town is east of Milan, which the Albion party chose as their base, making the ninety minute journey to Brescia by coach. As they made their final leg of the journey the snow began to fall, and it did not stop.

By the time of the kick off in Brescia's very open stadium, there was a thick carpet of snow on the pitch, and the locals had to delegate a team of sweepers to keep the touchlines clear as the two teams kicked off in a blizzard. Conditions were absolutely farcical, and the match – watched by a couple of hundred hardy fans, including a coachful from West Bromwich – would surely not have gone ahead in any other competition.

As happy as snowmen — the team in the blizzard in Brescia

"It was unreal, that was. We'd made the trip over, and the officials had gone over as well. The game was going to be called off, but they consulted the referee, and he said, 'No, let's get it played.' And on it went. I remember going out, and it was freezing, five or six inches deep in the end. It wasn't too deep at the start, but as the game went on, it got deeper and deeper, and we were all certain he would have to call it off. But they just wanted it out of the way, so we played on. When we went up and attacked, in their half, these guys would come on and try to clear the touchlines in our half, and then get off when Brescia attacked us – and then they would do the same at the top end.

Despite the farcical conditions, Bob scored the only goal. "The ball got put through and I ran onto it, but the ball was hardly moving. I kept kicking it as hard as I could to get it moving on the snow, and, to be honest, if the keeper had stopped where he was, I don't think I would have scored it, because I don't think I would have known what to do. But he came out so I just wellied it past him, and then sidefooted it as hard as I could towards goal. It just reached the goal, then started to gather snow, like a big snowball, and it just went a foot over the line. The strangest goal, the strangest game I ever played in. We had the orange ball, but because of the blizzard, coming straight into your eyes, you couldn't see the ball when it was in the air. A complete farce; but great fun! Behind the goal, afterwards, Strodds and some of the lads were chucking snowballs at the fans!"

Even more comical, as far as Albion fans were concerned, was the news that had come through about Stoke City's game in Italy. It had been called off, with a coachful of their fans stranded in deep snowdrifts, and because of Albion's win, which meant that Stoke could not qualify for the knock-out phase, their match was cancelled, never to be replayed, leaving the Potters' fans with an expensive wasted journey. All thanks to an 86th minute possibly offside goal from Bob!

The win earned Albion an 'English Semi-final' in the Anglo-Italian competition, and on January 30, on a night almost as cold as that in Brescia, Albion travelled the much shorter distance to St Andrews. On a bone-hard frozen surface, in front of just 9,113 shivering fans, Bob did not make the starting line-up, watching from the bench as his replacement, Tony Rees, led the line, and gave Albion an 18th minute lead. Gary Poole pulled Blues level and in the 59th minute Gary Bull put the home side ahead.

Bob came on in the 66th minute and fourteen minutes later Albion equalised, against the run of play, when Paul Raven powered home a Donovan corner. There was no further score in extra-time, which meant that the game – for only the fourth time in Albion's history — would be settled on penalties.

In a thrilling finish, Albion won their first-ever penalty shoot-out , 4-1, in front of the Albion fans at the Railway End. Bob duly put away his spot-kick, allowing an ex-Bluenose, David Smith, to score the decider.

The 'English Final' was a two-legged affair, and a competition which had started as a very low key affair had now become a very significant distraction, with the lure of a lucrative Final against an Italian side. Another League defeat at Ipswich, on February 3, sent Albion down to 23rd in the table. Bob, as mentioned previously, scored Albion's equaliser, and Andy Hunt missed a great chance to put his side ahead before Andy Mowbray scored an 80th minute winner. It did seem as if Albion's bad luck would never come to an end, and relegation looked a distinct possibility.

The dreadful run of results was finally ended with a win over Southend on February 10 – and Bob contributed to the 3-1 win with goals in the 46th and 86th minutes. That was a platform for a five game unbeaten run, interspersed with the two games against Port Vale in the Anglo-Italian English Final. The first leg, at The Hawthorns, ended goalless, but with away goals counting double, SuperBob went within five minutes of sending Albion to Wembley.

Jon McCarthy gave Vale a sixth minute lead, only for Bob to pull Albion level by heading his third goal in successive games. "It was an Ashcroft corner, I got a great leap, got up well, and when I headed it in – it was the equaliser, a few minutes from time – I thought, "Yes, Wembley, here we come!" Because you always want to play at Wembley, however many times you've been there. We'd done it with the Play-

So close, yet so far — Bob's header at Vale Park that nearly got Albion to Wembley

offs, but we wanted to get back there." If Albion could just hold out for the normal ninety minutes, extra time would not be required, for Albion would go through on away goals. As the game drew to a close, Albion's two thousand strong travelling fans began to anticipate a totally unexpected Wembley 'jolly,' until, five minutes from time, Ashcroft lost the ball in midfield and Vale swept upfield, Ray Walker crossing for Lee Glover to shoot home. Two minutes later, as Albion pressed desperately for an equaliser, they were caught out yet again as Martin Foyle volleyed home another cross from McCarthy, to dash Albion's Wembley dreams. Buckley was distraught. "When Bob scored, and we went into the last few minutes all square, I thought that was it. But I think it was written somewhere that Port Vale were going to Wembley; we didn't get what we deserved tonight." It would take all of Buckley's man management skills to raise his team's shattered confidence to face their looming two month battle against relegation.

Albion's brief unbeaten run in the League came to an end on March 9, when a 1-0 defeat at promotion-hunting Crystal Palace saw them drop back into 22nd place in the table. Things looked bleak indeed – until new Albion director, Paul Thompson, dug deep, and granted the club an interest-free loan to buy the player who eventually kept the club up. That man was former Ajax ace Richard Sneekes, who cost £400,000 from Bolton Wanderers. Sneekes had had to think long and hard about the move; so much so that he inserted a clause into his contract which would allow him to leave should Albion be relegated.

Bob — and the ball — in the net at Molineux in 1995-96

Bob was impressed with his new team mate — and the effect he had at his new club. "It was twelve games of unreal football. He's come from Bolton and I'd played against him a few times, so I knew what sort of player he was, but…well, if you wanted a player to make some sort of special impact, that was it. Not just with the players, but with the fans as well. His debut was Watford, when I scored my Albion hat-trick – but the game I really remember in that spell was at Leicester, when Richard scored that goal that stuck in the top of the net. That was unreal, that was!"

Sneekes made his debut against Watford at The Hawthorns on a cold, cold evening. Watford were in dire straits at the bottom of the table, but still had an outside chance of overhauling the teams above them, and the result was a thrilling encounter, that was a red-letter day for both Sneekes and SuperBob.

Albion scored first on 13 minutes when Bob seized on a poor clearance to shoot home from just inside the box. Debut boy Sneekes made it 2-0 three minutes later, and in the 27th minute Shane Nicholson turned Charlie Palmer inside out before crossing for Bob to fire home number three. Three goals up, Albion were coasting, but, true to form, they let Watford back into the game, the Hornets scoring twice in four minutes, through Ramage and Foster, to reduce Albion's lead at the break to a single goal.

Eleven minutes from the end of the game, Albion fans erupted when SuperBob steered home a pass from Sneekes to put Albion 4-2 up. At last, The Hawthorns Hero had scored a long-awaited hat-trick, his first in Albion colours. "We were 4-1 up at the time, then we draw the game 4-4, which you just can't believe." Even so, the match signalled an upturn in Albion's season. Barnsley were beaten 2-1, and then Albion fought for a 1-1 draw at St Andrews – which should have been a win. With Albion one up, Ian Hamilton hit the post and Bob followed up to put away the rebound, only for Blues defender Michael Johnson to keep the ball out with his hands. Referee Neil Barry, however, turned down Albion's appeals for a penalty and with ten minutes left, Jonathan Hunt equalised to deprive Albion of two vital points.

Sneekes had scored in both games, but it was Bob who scored Albion's point-saver in the return game at Watford, to take his tally to seven goals in eight games. Two more Sneekes goals ensured an unexpected win at Portsmouth, only for fellow relegation strugglers Luton Town to also win, unexpectedly, at The Hawthorns.

Next up, also at The Hawthorns, were Millwall. Remember, back in October, the two teams had met in much happier circumstances, with the winners going top of the table. It was that match which presaged the start of Albion's dreadful record-breaking losing sequence which had put them bottom of the table. Things had not gone too well for Millwall either, and, with another late winner from Sneekes, Albion's 1-0 win effectively relegated the Londoners. Three days later, Albion pulled off their astonishing win at promotion-chasing Leicester City, and played four more games unbeaten to rise to the dizzy heights of 14th in the table.

The last game of the season was at The Hawthorns, against already promoted Derby. The ground was full, as the fans turned up to celebrate Albion's escape. It was a special game for Bob, as well, in the end, as he went into the game on 99 goals in an Albion shirt. He was doubtful for the game for quite some time, having missed the previous two games with a hamstring injury, but he passed a pre-match fitness test and lined up alongside Andy Hunt.

And it was his strike partner who gave Albion a 13th minute lead with a spectacular thirty yard shot. That the goal was Hunt's first in eighteen games, went some way to explain why Albion had been struggling. Three minutes later, Dean Sturridge equalised with a blatantly offside goal, only for Richard Sneekes to score his tenth goal – in just thirteen games for the club – to put Albion ahead once more.

The scoreline remained at 2-1 to the Albion until two minutes from the end when the game, and the season, ended in a thrilling finale. It was then that Derby equalised, Ashley Ward scoring at the near post. The Rams thought they had got the draw – but SuperBob had other ideas. "I scored my hundredth goal for the Albion against Derby County at the end of that season. It might well have been offside, I don't know. People say that. All I know is that the ball was squared to me, and I put it into the net, and we won 3-2.

At the end of the game the fans invaded, and they lifted me onto their shoulders; it was nice, really, but I didn't celebrate that much to be honest. I think I knew what was coming, because the same thing had happened at Bristol when we got promoted. Both times we ended up in our slips..."

Thus Bob completed his century of goals, and Albion moved above both Blues and Wolves to finish in eleventh place; an amazing finish to a roller-coaster of a season that no Albion fan will ever forget. Had it not been for that incredible mid-season dip – or if Richard Sneekes had been signed a couple of months earlier – then Albion would surely have achieved a place in the Play-offs. Bob's record in such an up-and-down season was a remarkable one – 23 goals in 54 League and Cup games, a tally which saw him become only the twelfth player in Albion's history to top the one hundred goal mark.

Ray Harford... and Denis Smith

The summer of 1996 was one full of optimism for Bob Taylor, Albion and all of the club's fans. Bob had finished the '95-96 season in a rich vein of form with twelve goals in nineteen games, and he, along with Richard Sneekes, had helped to haul Albion from the bottom of the table to a respectable eleventh place in the First Division table.

Signing Sneekes was a masterstroke – if not by Buckley himself, then by the board, who had borrowed the money from new, in-coming director Paul Thompson – along with the loan transfer of Peter Butler. Both players were instrumental in helping Bob regain his sharpness in front of goal whilst, in turn, Sneekes fed off Bob's flick-ons and passes and had a great start to his Albion career. Thus Bob and the team prospered.

All seemed set fair. Over the summer Buckley had gone further to strengthen his squad, adding Paul Groves to the ranks. Signed from Buckley's old club, Grimsby, Groves was a utility player who had dominated the Mariners' side, but he would struggle to win over the fans in West Bromwich. Bob was sympathetic. "I felt sorry for Paul, because he was a good player, and he could have done a good job for the club at that time. What it was, Buckley had been buying a lot of players with a Grimsby connection, and Paul was the last of them. And I think by that time, the fans simply had enough of the Grimsby mob, because we were being nicknamed 'Grimsby Reserves.' Now, I can see why Buckley did it, because when you've got a team that's not quite gelling, you need to bring in someone you can trust, but I think he went a bit too far. The fans had had enough, and because they were on Paul's back from the first game, you're a marked man – and he'd had it then."

The Baggies' pre-season preparations took them to the Isle of Man where, in July 1996, they took part in the annual Isle of Man Football Festival, competing for the Manx Cup. In Albion's group were Port Vale and Wigan Athletic; Group A consisted of Bury, Wrexham and an Isle of Man XI. The Albion topped their group, beating the Valiants 2-0 – Bob notching his first pre-season goal – and Wigan 1-0, taking Albion to a Final against Bury at the Douglas Bowl. The only goal of the Final came in the 40th minute when Bob scored with a crisp, right-foot shot, after the Bury keeper had miskicked a goal kick straight to him. "We won the Cup in the Isle of Man. That was great, because I was still captain then, so I can say I collected a trophy as captain of the Albion! Bucko took us for a sight-seeing trip round the island, and we ended up in this boating pool, all of us in these little paddle-boats, and somehow somebody ended up in the pond, and then a lot of us ended up in the pond... It was fun; it was a bit of a laugh. We had a day off and all went off to the town centre and had a few beers." That, perhaps, made up for the poor accommodation they had on the island. "The hotel was bad; it was like a boarding house really, and we had to share three or four in a room. Fifty yards away there was a bowling alley with a club attached; I think a few of the lads went in there, but it was a bit risky; too close to home, if you know what I mean. Then we went to see the Port Vale lads, and they were in this plush luxury hotel on the seafront, and we were in this shitty little boarding house... And Port Vale were based in the centre of the island, at the International Stadium, but we had to travel all over the Isle of Man, up into the mountains and on the edge of a cliff, with no barriers on the roads – all to play in cowfields. It was unreal at times."

While the Albion party had been settling down in Douglas, the rest of the board had been busy finalising the £550,000 transfer of Paul Peschisolido from neighbours Birmingham City. The little Canadian had always been a thorn in the Albion side when playing against them for Blues and Stoke, and Buckley viewed the player as ideal competition for Taylor and Hunt for the two striking positions.

"Playing with Pesch was completely different to playing with Andy Hunt. Me and Andy seemed to gel together; we worked hard together and seemed to have some sort of an understanding and worked well together. Pesch was more of a lone-type striker, like Michael Owen is nowadays. Give him the ball, and with his pace and control, he could take on players and beat them.

Capt'n Bob, with Buckley and the Manx Cup

I wouldn't say he was difficult to play with, but I don't think we really clicked together on the pitch like me and Andy. But you can't knock him; he scored a few goals and the fans really took to him."

On August 2 Peter Butler finally signed for the Albion, Buckley paying Notts County £175,000 to convert a loan signing into a more permanent one, and ending a couple of month's uncertainty. This was supposedly the last piece of the jigsaw to help the club to the Premiership...

Despite all the talk of pressure on Bob and Andy, when the opening game of the season rolled around, their double act was still intact. But only because Peschisolido was suspended, because of a sending off the previous season in a stormy game against Wolves in the Birmingham Senior Cup. Whatever the reason, it was 'business as usual' for Hunt and Taylor against Barnsley and Colchester in the Coca-Cola Cup. On August 17 Albion kicked off the season against the Tykes at The Hawthorns, but in bright sunshine the Baggies turned in a dull performance to go down 2-1. Albion's goal came from a Hunt penalty, and Captain SuperBob, had, by his own admission, a poor game.

Three days later the Albion travelled to Layer Road to play Colchester, where three headed goals, from Hunt, Hamilton and Donovan gave them a 3-2 win. The following Saturday Bob got off the mark in the League, netting in the eleventh minute of the game against Charlton at The Valley, but once Carl Leaburn had equalised, it took some fine work by Nigel Spink, in the Albion goal, to keep the Londoners out.

It was a stuttering start – and it got worse, as little Colchester added another chapter to Albion's pathetic recent record in both cups, by winning the second leg of the Coca Cola Cup tie 3-1 at The Hawthorns, going through 5-4 on aggregate – even after losing their goalkeeper to injury, and playing a striker, former Blues player Steve Whitton, between the posts for the whole of the second half. Even the first appearance of Paul Peschisolido could not prevent a humiliating defeat.

After the game, Bob reflected ruefully on the experience. "The gaffer gave us a real rollicking; but what was said is best left private between us and him." Bob had been captain of the side since the start of the recovery the previous season – but this setback raised questions there, too. "We thought it was a lucky omen and I've remained captain ever since, but after the Colchester defeat I don't know whether I'll be asked to continue. The omens do not seem too good anymore." Buckley actually kept the players locked in the dressing room for 45 minutes after the game. While he was still captain, Bob felt it necessary to apologise to the fans. "Our fans deserve better and we are desperately sorry for letting them down. It was humiliating; we just did not turn up – and paid the penalty." And Bob paid the ultimate penalty for the defeat; he was dropped for the next game, as Andy

Hunt returned from injury to partner Peschisolido up front, away to recently relegated QPR. The shake-up seemed to have an effect, as Albion turned in a great performance – and Bob had the last word, coming on as substitute to score a late clinching goal in a 2-0 win. The goal was not enough to earn a recall for Bob, as for the next two games, Reading 3-2 (Hunt 3) and Wolves, Buckley stuck with Hunt and Pesch.

The game against the men from Molineux was another bad day as far as the Albion faithful were concerned. The first half was an abject display – compounded by being shown live on TV – with new goalkeeper Paul Crichton having a nightmare as the Wanderers strolled into a first half lead, with Bull and Iwan Roberts (twice) finding the net before Ian Hamilton pulled a goal back.

Bob replaced the ineffective Peschisolido at half time, and Dave Gilbert came on for Dave Smith – and between them, the two subs nearly saved the game, even after Roberts had completed a historic hat-trick. "I got one back, and then I had the one disallowed, when it wasn't offside. But then, maybe that made up for my hundredth goal against Derby being off-side; I don't know – swings and roundabouts, you know what I mean. Sometimes it evens itself out."

Yet worse was to come for Bob. During training the following Wednesday, he picked up an injury which was to have ramifications for his very future at the club. For some time, Albion's training facilities had been acknowledged as being well below standard. For the most part, the players trained at the Aston University Sports ground in Walsall, switching to The Hawthorns when the weather was bad and the pitches were unfit. The previous weekend, the Aston students had, as usual, been playing both football and rugby on the pitches, which were left rutted. "The pitch at Aston was really uneven, and I went over on my ankle, with all my weight, and I was out for a while then. It wasn't just that injury, though; I had footballers' ankle – it's like a baseball pitcher getting a stiff arm over the years. A twist-ed ankle is a common footballing injury, especially for strikers, who are turning all the time. You get the joints damaged, and a lot of crap – con-gealed dead blood, and so on – remains in the joint and calcifies, and it needs to be removed."

Richard Sneekes commented on the incident at the time. "Bob wasn't even tackled when he broke down with his injury. He was running one minute, and down the next. There was no-one to blame, and yet he's out for a month. I hope Bob recovers quickly because he is a great striker, and it made such a difference when he came on against the Wolves. He was pumped up after so many matches on the bench." Ominously, he continued, "Such is the nature of the game that many players go down – and never play again…"

Bob subsequently missed Albion's games against Tranmere, Ipswich, Oldham – when Paul Groves' late equaliser set up a new club record of twelve away games without defeat – and Huddersfield. He made his comeback on October 16, when Albion's miserable home form – in contrast to that on their travels – continued with a dreadful 2-0 home defeat against bogey side Stoke. To the watching Albion fans, it was patently obvious that Bob was unfit, but Buckley was almost pushed into playing him. Pesch, at the time, was playing for Canada in their World Cup qualifying games, which meant that the Albion boss only really had Hunt and Taylor to choose from.

In the last week of October, Bob admitted defeat in his immediate fight to regain full fitness, when the club announced that he would be out for another fortnight. It was clear that his injury was far worse than anyone thought, and its effects were legion, as Bob explained at the time. "It hurts when I run, it's sore when I shoot; and I'm turning about as sharply as the QE2. I came back as quick as I could, but the ankle still hurts and there's no point going out on the pitch if I cannot play my best for the gaffer and the rest of the team."

In Bob's absence, Albion won 3-2 at Swindon, stretching their unbeaten away run to an amazing fifteen games, with Paul Peschisolido scoring the goal of the season — and this just a short time after travelling nearly twenty hours back from a World Cup game in Panama. Bob's season was turning sour. On November 3 the team lost away from home at last, going down 4-0 at Portsmouth. The following week Bob made his first start since October 16, and celebrated with a goal, albeit one gifted to him after a collision between Vale keeper Paul Musselwhite and Dean Glover. The game ended 1-1 – which meant that Albion had won just two of their first nine home games – a record that did not improve when they lost to Sheffield United at The Hawthorns. By now, Buckley's 'lock-in' time had been extended to 62 minutes, as he vented his spleen in the dressing room.

Buckley knew he had hit a crisis, and with nine points from ten games, the press were questioning his tactics and his style of play. As for Bob, he was now alternating between the first team and the reserves, scoring for the Stiffs in a 3-2 win at Sunderland in the Pontins League, and hitting the winner in a Birmingham Senior Cup tie at Nuneaton. Back in the first team, it took a rare penalty for Bob to get on the scoresheet, against one of Bob's favourite teams, Bolton, after their keeper had flattened Pesch in the box, off the ball. With the season at the halfway stage, it was only Bob's fifth goal of the campaign.

A minute revival ensued over Christmas. Albion thumped Norwich City 5-1, then played out a 3-3 draw with Oxford – a match which epitomised Albion's whole season. The game was goalless for the first 33 minutes, when a misunderstanding between Julian Darby and Paul Crichton left Jemson with an open goal. Ten minutes later Sneekes equalised and right on half time Andy Hunt put Albion ahead from the spot. Two goals in four minutes from Murphy and Elliott saw Oxford ahead with eight minutes remaining. There was still time for Andy Hunt to miss a penalty and, in injury time, for Bob to run in an equaliser after Hamilton had hit the post. The match finished in chaos, with the crowd on the pitch, Hunt and Oxford keeper Phil Whitehead exchanging blows, unseen by the referee, and Oxford manager Denis Smith angrily remonstrating with the fourth official on the touchline. Rarely can a Bob Taylor goal have caused such pandemonium.

The revival continued with a draw at Reading, and a splendid 4-1 win over QPR, before lowly Tranmere visited The Hawthorns on New Year's Day, and left with all three points. The writing was on the wall for Alan Buckley, particularly after a three goal drubbing at Chelsea in the third round of the FA Cup. On Sunday January 12 any patience the fans had finally snapped in the return encounter with the Wolves at Molineux. Once again, the match was televised, once again, Bob was on the bench and, sadly, once again, Albion were humiliated. By the break, when, once again, Bob replaced Pesch, Albion were two goals down. This time there would not be even the hint of a comeback, and Buckley's days were numbered.

The following Wednesday Bob had a run-out for the Reserves in a Birmingham Senior Cup tie against Aston Villa, at The Hawthorns. The match had a novelty value in that it was being broadcast live – on local cable TV, and, thanks to a successful penalty from Bob in the shoot-out, Albion went through into the semi-final. Bob had had a good game, and was back in the first team for the home game against struggling Oldham. Just 12,000 people saw Bob open the scoring with a splendid overhead kick, only for Stuart Barlow to peg the Albion back, and send Albion down to 17th in the table, seven points above the relegation zone. He did not know it at the time, but Bob had scored the last goal of the 'Buckley era'.

On Wednesday January 22 chairman Tony Hale dismissed the manager. "He was the right man when we appointed him, and he kept us up, but when it comes to guiding us to the Premier League, Alan lost his way somewhere." As Bob recalled, John Trewick took charge again. "Then we lost 5-0 at Ipswich. We stopped at a hotel and the bus broke down, and we had to get taxis to the ground. It was a great excuse though, wasn't it, after the game; the bus broke down, and we were all over the place! Then we played Blues, and we heard that Ray Harford was watching in the stand, because the rumours had been going round. I scored two good headers that day. I don't think we were playing particularly well, and we went a goal down, but we got a corner and there was a big melee, and my head just popped up, and I seemed to hover there. I didn't get a particularly good connection, and there was a lad on the post, but the ball looped over him. That made it 1-1, then we went 2-1 down and Richard Sneekes made it 2-2. We needed to steady the ship at that point, and a 2-2 draw was good for us, but late on – in the 89th minute – Andy Hunt put over this great cross, looping and hanging. The keeper was backtracking, Ablett was on a standing jump and the full-back was coming in behind him, but they ended up three together. I attacked the ball at the far stick and the three of them ended up in the net, with the ball! I rushed over to the Albion fans, one of those silly spur of the moment things, kissing the badge. It was an important win, and very good for me, from a personal point of view, in front of the new manager."

The following day former Blackburn Rovers coach Ray Harford was named as the new manager, with John Trewick as his assistant, and Cyrille Regis as first team coach. Harford had had an unspectacular playing career, serving Charlton, Exeter, Lincoln, Mansfield, Port Vale and Colchester, but had risen to prominence as an innovative coach, and helped Kenny Dalglish take Blackburn to the Premier League title.

Bob had obviously impressed his new boss with the two goals at the Blues, and he played in eleven of the next thirteen games, his best run of the season. yet he netted just one goal in that run, the winner in a good 2-1 win at Bramall Lane on April 5. With his ankle giving him so much trouble, he was clearly not the Bob of old, and with two games of the season remaining, and Albion's safety assured after a goalless draw at the McAlpine Stadium, he had the operation that he had needed all season.

It was Ray Harford who finally made the decision for him. "Bob has been putting the operation off bravely for weeks on end. He had intended playing until the very end of the season, but it was time for something to be done." Harford's assistant, John Trewick, was fulsome in his praise of his fellow Geordie. "Bob has given one hundred percent throughout the season, but he has never been totally fit. He has done a great job for the team over the weeks, despite lacking fitness; with Peschisolido away so often he hung on so we would have cover."

Bob remembers it slightly differently. "Ray was playing Pesch when he was available, and me when Paul had to go off to play for Canada in the World Cup – which he was doing at regular intervals at that point. When Pesch was playing, I would be on the bench. I delayed it and delayed it, but I couldn't have the operation with Pesch being away with Canada every three weeks. But the manager wouldn't let me have it done because we hadn't got another striker to replace Pesch. In the end I got the ankle cleaned out. Normally they would use two or three litres of water to clean the ankle out, but in mine there was so much crap that he was using six or seven litres. And then the surgeon found an ulcer in there, and they had to get that out as well."

All told, that season, Bob had started just sixteen League games, plus another sixteen as substitute, but had still managed to contribute a vital ten goals, as well as leaving Albion fans with two unforgettable performances, the second half against the Wolves when he had tried, almost single-handedly, to pull the game back out of the fire, and his two goal blast at St Andrews, which has gone down in Baggies folklore.

As a final reward for his efforts, that winner at Blues earned Bob the Supporters Club's *Goal of The Season* Award. He now had all summer to recuperate from his ankle operation – but, sadly, things would get very much worse for Bob, before they would get better.

The sorceror and his apprentice; Bob Taylor and Lee Hughes

Trigger joins the Trotters

During the summer of 1997, Ray Harford almost upset the Albion applecart by threatening to resign because of the board's intransigence over transfers, particularly with regards to the close attention that new director Paul Thompson was paying to the situation. Anxious not to lose their highly rated coach, the board backed down somewhat, and put forward the money for Kevin Kilbane, Albion's first million pound signing. The youngster, who cost £1.25m from Preston, was a Republic of Ireland Under-21 international, and was seen as an ideal provider for the likes of Hunt, Pesch and Taylor. Albion, after persistent pressure from John Trewick, had also signed young Kidderminster hot-shot Lee Hughes, a youngster who was viewed at the time as a signing for the future. However, Peschisolido was soon in a contractual dispute with the club. His agent Eric Hall was conducting negotiations, and his robust style was not going down too well with the board. The episode would end with Peschisolido's departure for Fulham, for a million pounds – a move which had the blessing of Harford, who saw Peschisolido's Canadian jaunts as disruptive to the side.

That left Albion with two experienced strikers, and a tyro; surely Bob's season was set fair, particularly once his ankle problem had settled down after the operation. Alas, it never got the chance. "That summer was the hottest on record. I had a tough training programme, and then some run-outs in pre-season friendlies; but they were all played on dry, bone-hard surfaces, which did my ankle no good at all. It was bone scraping on bone, and I was in agony, and it never got a rest at all."

When the League season kicked off on August 9, Bob was already sidelined, and he missed the promising opening day win against Tranmere, when Kilbane celebrated with a debut goal. In fact, Bob missed the first five League and Cup games, and it was not until the last day of August that he made his first appearance, in a 1-1 draw at Ipswich. He did, however, play in six of the next nine games, but, ominously, only got on the scoresheet once, with Albion's equaliser in a 1-1 draw in the Coca Cola Cup at Kenilworth Road.

By now, Harford had built a tight, disciplined unit at The Hawthorns, and on September 6, they went top of the First Division table – for the first time since 1989 – with a 1-0 home win over Reading. Bob, though, was way below his best, and by mid-October he was in the Reserves; not a pleasant experience at any time.

Albion's Reserve side was a poor one; after winning their opening fixture, they had gone seven games without a win, and it took all of Bob's experience – with a couple of goals – to help break that sequence with a win over Coventry City. Sadly, though, even at that level, the injury meant that Bob still looked short of pace, and badly lacking in match-fitness.

His season was rapidly turning into a nightmare, and, indeed, Bob's crown was slipping, as 'the young pretender,' Lee Hughes, had got off to an unexpectedly good start to his full-time career, scoring loads of goals from the subs' bench. Bob himself was most impressed by the youngster. "He was raw! We trained together, and he was a great natural finisher. The ball would be all over the place, and ricochets everywhere, but somehow he'd get on the end of it, and put it away. I thought "Bloody Hell!" And when I found out he was actually a winger at Kidderminster... One day he came up to me in training and said 'Bob, I used to be on the terraces singing your name!' He was a natural scorer, and a Baggie born and bred, and he went from strength to strength, and he's got where he wanted to be. This season's been a bit different for him, of course, but he's earned a fair bit – and earned a fair bit for the club. They paid what? £250,000 for him from Kidderminster, then sold him for £5m – and they got him back on the cheap. They can't complain."

There was more pressure put on Bob when Harford signed centre-forward Mickey Evans from Southampton for £750,000; perhaps, with his contract up at the end of the season, it was time for Bob to reconsider his future at the club. He thought otherwise. "I have been here for nearly six years and I want to stay here for the rest of my career. I am not the type to storm into the manager's office and make an issue of not being in the side. I won't be packing my bags. I want to be part of Albion's plans. The way the side has been playing means that the boss will want to keep the same side; I've just got to keep plugging away and hope I can do something to impress the manager."

Bob never got the chance. On December 4 Ray Harford walked out on the club, citing 'personal reasons.' Stunned Albion fans soon heard the rumour that Harford was expected to take over at QPR, and for a time, a livid Tony Hale took out an injunction to prevent his employee moving in at Loftus Road. John Trewick, once again, took over as caretaker, and a dispirited Albion lost two of the next three games. Bob got back into the side for a 2-0 home defeat by Huddersfield, just before Christmas; it was only his fourth League game of the season.

Bob had been a big fan of Harford's when he arrived. "Ray Harford was really laid back. I don't think he ever got really ANGRY angry, if you know what I mean; he just knew how to put things right. Training was great; he could turn a shooting session into an eleven-a-side training game.

That's how he did it, and it was fantastic to watch, and to be involved."

Bob's opinion of the coach changed when he was preparing to leave. "In the end, when he left, he put it down to all the travelling, from his house down south. Perhaps I was being selfish at the time, but I remember thinking that he had coped perfectly well with the travelling when he was at Blackburn, which was two hours further down the road. He didn't tell us what the real reason was, and we all thought, 'He's shit on us.' He had a meeting with all the lads, to tell them about it, and I refused to go to it. I thought we were going to go up that season, and I was really enjoying it. Mind you, even when we were doing well, he was hardly coming in. We wouldn't see him on Monday and Tuesday, he'd come in on Wednesday, maybe we'd see him on Thursday – he left John Trewick to take the training then – and then we wouldn't see him again until the match on the Saturday. But we were doing well, and he didn't need to be there. Then a couple of results started to go astray. It was a disappointment; especially as he'd left to go to QPR, which wasn't a bigger club than us, and wasn't doing what we were doing."

The club appointed Stoke City man Denis Smith as the new manager. Smith had been a Potteries legend as a tough centre-half with Stoke, and had had a successful managerial career with York, Sunderland and Oxford. Ironically, he had taken over at Bristol City just weeks after the Robins had sold Bob to the Albion in February 1992; but he and Bob just never hit it off.

"I was doing some extra training on my own, just doing shuttle-runs and 'doggies' – just trying to get fit, to get back on level par with the rest of the lads. Denis came over and said 'Somebody's told me you're overweight, slow, and you like a drink.' I asked him to tell me who had told him that. He wouldn't tell me – and then said he wanted me to go out on loan – 'to see me play.' I couldn't believe it. I'd played three or four hundred games for the Albion, and against Smith's

Left, Alan Buckley, right, Denis Smith

95

teams many a time, so I couldn't understand why he needed to see me play. So I got the impression my face didn't fit. I told him I wanted to stay at the Albion, get fit and fight for my place."

But Smith was persistent. "For four or five days after that, he kept ringing me at home, about going on loan. At the end I got sick of it, and I had Lesley answering the phone for me, and telling him I was out. In the end, he said 'Oxford want you on loan, how about that.' As if it was all done and dusted – and I still said no! He tried that two or three times, and I kept saying no. Then he rang again, and he said, 'Well, you'll not turn THIS one down, will you; it's a Premiership club – Bolton want you on loan, and I suggest you take it.' I couldn't believe it. I told him I'd ring him back in five minutes, and I had a word with Lesley. She told me to go for it, because she knew I'd always wanted to play in the Premiership. And in that five minutes Colin Todd rang me, and explained the situation. So I agreed, went back to the Albion and signed the papers to go to Bolton for a month, and that was that."

Bob moved straight from the Pontins League, to the Premier League! With Bolton struggling at the bottom of the table, in their first season back in the big time, manager Colin Todd swooped to sign Bob on a month's loan, as cover for the injured Dean Holdsworth, starting with the relegation clash against Southampton at the Reebok Stadium. "There are no guarantees, but he knows the job I am asking him to do. He is a strong player and should take some of the weight off Nathan Blake's shoulders," said Todd. SuperBob's Premier League debut ended in a 1-1 draw, and he played in the Trotters' next three games, a 2-1 defeat by Newcastle at St James', a 5-1 hammering by Coventry and, on February 7, the highlight of the season, against Manchester United at Old Trafford. What a great stage on which to score your first-ever goal in the top flight of English football. It came after sixty minutes, and gave Bolton the lead. "It was another close range one, but it was the Busby Babes Memorial day, they had wreaths on the pitch, and it was a memorable day — a 1-1 draw. Later, I was told that it was my goal that sparked the rift between Andy Cole and Teddy Sheringham – I shared an agent with Teddy, and got to know Teddy pretty well, and there was some sort of row over the fact that one of them should have been marking me that day. And the row continues to this day; all down to me! Barry Neville is Teddy's agent, and when I was at Bolton, John Salako came in, and Barry was his agent as well, and he took me on as well, and it was he who told me about the row."

On the same day, Albion had won 2-0 at Swindon, and their fans, coming back on the coaches from the County Ground, cheered long and loud when the news of Bob's goal came over the radio. A week later,

Bob was back at The Hawthorns, as sub against Ray Harford's Queens Park Rangers. It was a stormy game, with Harford jeered as he got off the team coach in Halfords Lane – and jeered all through the game as well. Such were the concerns for his safety that he had two minders who stood by the Rangers' dug-out throughout the game.

Bob came on in the second half, as a substitute for Franz Carr. He certainly looked a lot sharper after his 'triumph' at Old Trafford, but still missed a hat-trick of chances as the game ended 1-1 – with the Brummie Road's new idol, Lee Hughes, scoring the welcome equaliser.

Bob was back in the side for the next match at Oxford and, at last, he scored his first League goal of the season, set up by Lee Hughes, in a 2-1 defeat. He still did not have the confidence of his manager, who promptly went out and signed another striker, Northern Ireland international James Quinn, paying Blackpool £500,000 for his services. Yet Bob then had his best run in the first team, playing in the next seven games. On March 21 he came on as a sub against Port Vale, and scored, in what would prove to be the last game of his seven year stay at the Albion. During that week, he had been transfer-listed, along with Andy Hunt and Paul Holmes, after failing to agree a contract with the club.

"I had Des Bremner to come in from the PFA to represent me. That day Des went in, and he'd had the meeting set for 10 a.m. I was due in for training at 10 as well, and at 10.10 Des arrived at the training ground! I went over to him and asked why he hadn't been to the meeting. "I have. I sat down, and before I said anything, John Wile said 'We're offering Bob a one year deal, take it or leave it, or he's on the transfer list.'" And I said, 'I take it I'm on the transfer list, then?' Obviously Des and I had already discussed that I wanted a three year deal to take me to my Testimonial, and Wile was nowhere near it. It was just the arrogance of the man that got me."

On transfer deadline day, Bob had a meeting with Smith. "Denis told me he wanted me to stay, so I told him it was up to him to sort it out with the board. He told me he wanted me, then said, 'But by the way, the board had already accepted £50,000 from Bolton for you to go on loan with them until the end of the season.' So all the time he was telling me that he wanted me to stay, he knew that the board had negotiated for me to go! That's what got me. It wasn't so much about staying then. I said, 'Right, bollocks! It's all done and dusted – I'm going training.' I met Denis outside afterwards and when he asked me what I was doing, I just said, "Right, I'm going to Bolton!"

Bob spoke to the press with some bitterness at the time. "I should be going to Bolton with real enthusiasm. This is a great chance for any player, and I enjoyed my month up there. But to be honest, I would rather be at the Albion. I love the place, and I wanted to end the season there. I don't know what the future holds for me now. The way things are going, I could be on the dole at the end of the season. I have given part of my life to the club, and it has ended like this."

And so Bob moved north to Lancashire, on a mission to save Bolton Wanderers from the drop. He played in eight of their last nine games, scoring the winner at home to Blackburn Rovers in a 2-1 win on April 11. Two weeks later, he cheered Bolton and Albion fans alike with a goal in Bolton's 3-1 win at Villa Park. He had been ribbed mercilessly by the home fans for 41 minutes, when he put his side 2-0 up with a glorious strike which left the Holte End stunned – and Bob dancing with delight.

"I started the game at the Villa, and I had a lot of friends there. I enjoyed it, but I was getting such a lot of stick from the Holte End, in particular, because of the Albion thing. Then Neil Cox scored, and we went 1-0 up. I remember Dwight Yorke having the ball on the halfway line, and trying to square it to Scimeca. I slid in, and dragged the ball away, and Scimeca fell over the ball. I ran on forty or fifty yards with the ball, until I came up to Gareth Southgate. I think I was so knackered by then, I didn't know what to do, so I just hit it. It went past Gareth on the outside of him, and it went in on Bosnich's near post. He should never have let it in, because he was only a couple of yards off his near post, and it was a daft shot to try for – but in it went. And the whole Holte End went quiet. And I went mad. "Aaarghh!" — like a mad Zulu! I ran down the touchline, doing high fives with all the coaching staff. It shut them up – but there was a round of applause as well. We had a bit of trouble after that, and they pulled a goal back, but Nathan Blake scored again, and we won 3-1."

However, the season ended in failure. Despite a 5-2 win over Crystal Palace the week after, Bolton went down on the last day of the season. They lost 2-0 at Chelsea but, more significantly – and oddly – Everton pulled back a two goal deficit against Wimbledon to win 3-2, and save themselves at Bolton's expense. The Toffees finished level on points with Bolton, and stopped up because they had scored five more goals than the Trotters...

In addition, earlier in the season, Gerry Taggart had scored a perfectly good goal for Bolton at Everton, which had been disallowed because the referee had not realised that the ball had come back into play after going into the net. It was that decision which doomed Bolton, as much as any shenanigans by Hans Segers in the Wimbledon goal...

Bob's brush with the Premier League was over, but the Bolton fans had taken to him as one of their own, and Colin Todd was impressed enough to offer him a contract – so Bob wouldn't be back on the dole, and playing snooker again, after all!

Wembley once more

During the close season, Bob, and his agent, thrashed out the details of his contract at Bolton. "Colin Todd and the Bolton chairman had said they'd look after me. I used Barry Neville, the first time I had ever bothered with an agent, and we met at Teddy Sheringham's house to discuss how we would handle things with Bolton, and it was all done within a couple of days."

Once that was all sorted, Bob went off on holiday, and came back refreshed for pre-season training with his new club, before leaving on the club's pre-season tour of Ireland. Bob was well aware of the competition he would be facing with so many quality strikers already at the Reebok. "I played a few games in Ireland, and I scored a few goals, and got myself into the team, but we had quite a few strikers there then. There was me, Dean Holdsworth, Nathan Blake, Arnar Gunnlaugsson and, when we were in Ireland, we took a lad who had come over on trial, Eidur Gudjohnsson. I was mostly sub in Ireland, but I scored three or four goals, and felt fitter."

Bob kept his house in Lichfield, and commuted to Bolton, which was an easy ninety minute journey, stopping up there in a hotel before matches. He started the season on the bench, but, three days later, played his first game – and scored his first goal – in a 1-0 win over Hartlepool, with whom he had had trials many years before, in a first round first leg Worthington Cup game. "The one thing about Bolton was the number of foreign players. I never played with that many foreign players elsewhere, but at Bolton there were South African internationals, Danish internationals, Icelandic internationals, Norwegian internationals. And Peter Beardsley was there, a real hero of mine. Even at 35-36, he was still a brilliant player. And there were lads that I knew from my Leeds days, like John Sheridan and Scott Sellars, and I knew Neil Cox, from the Villa, so I knew a lot of them."

Bob made his first League appearance as a substitute in a disappointing 2-2 draw at home to Sheffield United. Ten days later, he was on the bench again, for one of the most important games of the season, as far as he was concerned. "My return to The Hawthorns. I was very nervous, because I didn't know how people would react, the first time back. Still living in the area, I knew that there had been some unrest about the way I'd gone, but I hadn't spoken to the papers to give my version of it, so I was worried. And I didn't think I'd ever come back to the Albion the way I did. People say that I knew I'd be back, but I didn't. I remember I bought Mo – the lady who washes the kit — some flowers, because I got on really well with the groundstaff and so on, but I'd never really had the chance to say goodbye. And when I got up to come on; the reception I got was unbelievable. You're standing there, and there's all this noise; incredible. In the end, it was almost embarrassing, and I just wanted to get on the pitch. We won the game, when we were down to ten men, and people still ask me if I played for the free kick from which Riccardo Gardner scored the winner – a bit of a sucker punch, really."

It was not only Bob who was astonished by the warmth of his reception from his many Albion fans. "At the end of the game I was sitting in the dressing room. Now, Bolton is a real friendly sort of club, and the chairman would regularly come into the dressing room after games, for a chat, to lift you if you'd lost, or celebrate if you'd won. And the chairman came over to me and told me that he'd never seen anything like it in his time in football – he'd never seen such a reception from both sets of fans. Because I had a really good thing with the Bolton fans as well. I don't know why they took to me so well; it was the same at Bristol as well. I honestly don't know why. There was a big thing about the welcome I had in the Bolton evening paper as well; the reporter there had never seen anything like it either."

Nathan Blake had picked up an injury at The Hawthorns, so Bob was in the Bolton side for their next game, at home to Birmingham City. The last time that Bob had played against the Blues, in John Trewick's last game as caretaker-manager of the Albion, in 1997, he had scored two cracking goals. He repeated that feat for Bolton. "It was my first game back in the side, properly, and I was really worked up for that game, I went in on Ablett, we collided, and I put away the loose ball – after just seventeen seconds of the game! I scored a second goal early in the second half, and we won 3-1."

The following week Bob kept his place, even though Blake was fit again, and scored another goal, in a thrilling 4-4 draw at Gresty Road. It was not enough to keep his place again the week after, when top scorer Blake returned to the side, leaving Bob on the sidelines for three weeks. But Bob's time would come; Nathan Blake was attracting a lot of attention from Premiership clubs, and at the end of October, cash-strapped Bolton finally succumbed, much against the wishes of manager Colin Todd, and sold the striker – who had already scored nine goals – to Blackburn Rovers for £4.25m.

Bob grabbed his chance with both hands. On November 4, in the first game after Blake's departure, Bob opened the scoring for

Bolton after just five minutes against Port Vale, as his side won 3-1. Two weeks later came two crucial away wins, in the space of four days, both by 1-0 scorelines, at Ipswich and Stockport – and it was Bob who scored both the goals. He then followed that up with goals in two 1-1 draws, at Tranmere and Wolverhampton – making it five goals in six games – as Bolton climbed up the table to fifth place. "The goal at Molineux was a bit of a contentious goal as well. The ball was put over the top, and Dean Richards came in, and either he hit it against me, or I hit it against him, but either way it went in, and they were saying it might have been an own goal. I don't care, as long as it went in. But they scored a controversial equaliser as well."

On Saturday February 13, it was Albion's turn to visit the Reebok, the first time that they had played at Bolton since the move from Burnden Park. Under Denis Smith, Albion had got off to a good start to the season, thanks almost entirely to the stunning goalscoring form shown by Lee Hughes. By the time Albion came to Bolton, the side had peaked, and had dropped down to eighth place in the table, but Hughesie had already scored an amazing 28 goals – eighteen more than Bob!

It was a massive day for SuperBob. Before the game, he had a word with Hughesie, and asked if he could swap shirts with him after the final whistle, because he didn't have an Albion 'home' shirt at home. "I was asked before the game what I would do if I scored,. And I said – 'Nothing!' I knew I wouldn't want to celebrate, because I wouldn't want to rub the noses of the fans who had supported me six or seven years, and try to embarrass them, because they deserved better."

Albion got off to a good start in a game they knew they needed to win to keep in with a chance of a Play-off place. In the 27th minute, former Bolton striker Fabian De Freitas shot Albion ahead, against the run of play. Bolton poured forward, constantly channeling the ball down the Albion left, and it was from that source that Bolton equalised, in first half injury time. Bob had already had a goal disallowed for offside, but he got the goal he had been looking for when he drifted away from Paul Holmes to cleverly volley in Per Frandsen's long cross. True to his word, he did not celebrate the goal, quietly walking back upfield and, a few moments later, back into the dressing room.

Six minutes into the second half, Bolton won the game – and went second in the table – when Neil Cox nudged a close range effort over the line, with the Albion defence in disarray. Albion, controversially, were robbed of a point near the end when Lee Hughes twice forced the ball over the goal line, only for the referee and his assistant to both miss the incident.

At the final whistle, Bob duly swapped shirts with Hughes, to the appreciation of the travelling supporters. "I wasn't being patronizing when I swapped shirts and kissed the badge, because I'd never really had the chance to say goodbye to the supporters; I'd sort of sailed out into the sunset when I left the Albion. I couldn't shake hands with all of them, or write to all of them, so this was the next best thing. It was my way of saying how much I loved the club, and appreciated the fans' support."

Above: Bob evades Paul Holmes to put Bolton level against the Albion at the Reebok.
Facing page, Bob signals his appreciation of the Albion fans at the final whistle

Albion's season never really recovered, and, after heavy defeats at Birmingham, Sunderland and at home to Crewe, they ended the season in 12th place – a finish that would, eventually, cost Denis Smith his job. Strangely, after the success against the Albion, Bolton's season also took something of a downturn, and they only won one of the next ten games; that win was against QPR, and Bob scored both goals, his thirteenth and fourteenth of the season, which nudged him just ahead of Dean Holdsworth as the club's top scorer.

Eventually, Bolton seemed almost to stumble into the last Play-off place, just nipping in ahead of the Wolves by virtue of a last day win at Portsmouth, and Wolves' shock home defeat by Bradford City. City's win had also deprived Ipswich Town of an automatic promotion place, after leading the race all season, and it was the Suffolk side – who had contested the Play-off for four years in a row without success — that Bolton had to meet in the Play-off semi-finals.

Bolton won the first leg game at the Reebok on May 16, but only thanks to a Johansen goal six minutes from time. Three days later, the two teams met again in the second leg at Portman Road. "We knew that they would be hard to beat on their pitch, where they could pass it around, and they had the likes of Kieran Dyer, David Johnson and Matty Holland. It was always going to be a hard game, and when we went a goal down after about fifteen minutes, they really got their tails up then."

Somehow, Bolton managed to hold out until the break, and six minutes into the second half, Bob scored a vital away goal. "I equalised, and it was 1-1 early in the second half. They scored again straight away, through Kieran Dyer, then Per Frandsen scored for us to make it 2-2, five minutes from the end." Just when it looked as if Bob was back at Wembley, Dyer struck again in injury time, to level the aggregate at 3-3, and send the game into extra time.

An incredible topsy-turvy game still had more turns. Six minutes into the first period of extra time, Bob scored his second goal, to put Bolton 4-3 ahead on aggregate – and effectively killed off the tie. It meant that, because of Bolton's four away goals, Ipswich had to score twice more in extra time. Even so, the last four minutes of the game were excruciating, as Matt Holland made it 4-3 to Ipswich on the night, but the Trotters held out to reach the Final. In the other tie, Watford had beaten Birmingham City 7-6 on penalties, after each side had won their home game 1-0, so it was Graham Taylor's men that Bob would face at Wembley on the last day of May.

There were other things to think about on that evening of celebration, as Bob recalls. "The sad thing about that night was that a father and his son died in a car crash on the way from Bolton to that game. All the Bolton players went to the funeral, and the widow and the family were VIP guests with us at Wembley."

There was to be no happy return to Wembley for Bob. He had enjoyed his success there with Albion six years before, but this time Bolton were never in the game. Watford won it – and their brief spot in the Premiership – with goals in each half from Nick Wright and Allan Smart. "The Watford game at Wembley was awful. It's the one day in football when I think I've cried, because I really thought I was going into the Premiership. That was my last time playing at Wembley, and I enjoyed the day, but it was awful when we lost. Well, I've won one, and lost one there." Bob ended the season as Bolton's top scorer – to complete 'the set' of Bolton, Albion and Bristol City – with a creditable eighteen goals, four goals ahead of Arnar Gunnlaugsson.

Things would never be the same for Bob at the Reebok. "The following season I wasn't in the team so much at Bolton. I had a bit of a knee operation at the start of that season. I'd nicked my cartilage in the Play-off Final against Watford, and it needed sorting, so I had it slightly trimmed. I went through pre-season with it, and then had it done, and ended up missing a month. It was the same old thing, playing catch-up again with the other players. It was the same old déjà vu – and I thought 'here we go again.'"

It was to be a stunning season for Bolton, in which they would reach the semi-finals of both domestic cup competitions and reach the Play-offs again, but Bob, because of his injury, was often a bit player. Once again, he got off the mark for the season in the Worthington Cup, scoring one of his side's goals in a 5-3 win against Darlington. That got him back into the League side, for the home game with Barnsley on September 18. The following week, the Bolton board went above Colin Todd's head to sell Per Frandsen to Blackburn for £1.75m. The manager resigned on September 22, and his replacement – the former Bolton star, Sam Allardyce – was appointed four weeks later.

It would be some time before Bob could get back into the starting line-up under the new manager, although he did notch his first goal in the League when he scored the opening goal from the bench, in a 2-0 home win against Swindon. "Sam Allardyce took over, and he said he'd speak to everybody, but he never spoke to me about contracts, and I got the impression that he was just going to leave it and leave it, until my contract ran out in the summer."

Bob scored two more goals in the League under Allardyce, both at the Reebok, first in a 3-2 home defeat by Tranmere, and then in a 2-0 home win against Portsmouth. By then, Bolton were fighting on three fronts, and Bob was playing his part in both cups. In the first leg of the Worthington Cup semi-final, Bolton went down to another home defeat by struggling Tranmere, and then were hammered in the second leg. "I was sub in the Worthington Cup semi-final second leg match against Tranmere. I came on, but by then we were 2-0 down, and we lost 3-0, and it was too late."

There was still the FA Cup; and Bob played in every game, right up to the quarter final. It was his two goals in a 3-1 win at Cambridge United that put Bolton into the sixth round, where they scraped through 1-0 against First Division runaway leaders Charlton. That gave them a semi-final place against Aston Villa, to be played at Wembley. It looked as if Bob might have at least one more chance of glory at the old Stadium, just before it was scheduled for demolition.

"Then I got the call. From Mick Phelan. He asked me if I wanted to come back to the Albion, and I said yes straight away. No need to ask for time to think about it; I said yes. Mick Phelan is a big pal of Gary Megson, by the way, and he was at Manchester United at that time. I said yes, then I thought about it, and thought, 'Shit, what have I done?' But as I told everybody at the time – 'No regrets.' I hadn't been brought in just to keep Albion up. If we did stay up, then great, but if we went down, so be it. The deal was done in a matter of days, once Barry Neville had spoken to the gaffer. They offered me three and a quarter years, and a testimonial – at last! What I couldn't get the first time round, I got the second!"

Realistically, Bob was trading a chance of Wembley and Premiership glory for the chance of continuing his career for another three seasons at the club he loved. "I knew I wasn't going to get another contract at Bolton, but we were in for promotion, and in for a chance of the FA Cup Final in the last one ever at Wembley, before they knocked it down. But I joined the Albion the week before the semi-final."

Financially, there was a big difference between the two clubs. "There was a big drop in wages. Even when I went to Bolton, they offered me more wages than here, but it wasn't massive, massive, because Bolton had got their troubles. They'd built the new ground, but they couldn't sell the old one, and they were laying off people when I went there, and they were in administration. But by the time I came back here, I took a big, big drop in wages. But you don't just play for the money. And I got the Testimonial, because I could have had two years at the Albion, on the same money I was on at Bolton, or three and a bit years, on much lower wages, plus a Testimonial. It was ten years, and I wanted ten years at the club."

The move had cost the Albion £100,000 – less than two years after the club had 'given away' Bob for nothing. It turned out to be the best value Albion have ever had.

Back to The Hawthorns

The 1999-2000 season was a bizarre and troublesome one for the Albion. After squeaking through an EGM during the summer, chairman Tony Hale sacked manager Denis Smith four days before the start of the League season. He then paid £50,000 to Stoke to get Brian Little in early as the new boss, and Albion went a club record thirteen games without defeat from the start of the season before things started to fall apart. By Christmas, Albion were in the bottom six, Tony Hale had been ditched, and replaced by Paul Thompson in an amazing boardroom clear-out that saw five directors lose their seats on the board. On March 4, having guided Albion to just five League wins in the 34 games in which he was in charge, Brain Little was sacked by Thompson after an extraordinary outburst following a heavy home defeat by Birmingham City.

Within a week, the Albion appointed out of work Gary Megson – late of Blackpool, Stoke and Stockport – to the hottest seat in football. He got off to a sensational start, when Lee Hughes scored in the first minute of his first game, to win a tricky match at Stockport, but that was followed by a disappointing home defeat by Huddersfield which saw the side drop into the bottom four.

On Tuesday March 22, Albion lost 2-0 at Portsmouth. In a fiery game, Albion conceded a nonsensical penalty, had Matt Carbon sent off, and failed to get a shot on target all night. Even Gary Megson was in the wars, banished from the touchline after abusing referee Graham Poll. It was only Megson's third game in charge since taking over, and his comment on the performance was, "totally indefensible!" The result left the manager with no illusions over the nature of the task he had taken on, as Albion slipped down the table, just one point ahead of third-from-bottom Walsall. He had already decided that new faces were needed; little did Albion's fans realise that one of those new faces would be a familiar 'old' one...

On transfer deadline day, March 24, Megson signed Georges Santos, paying Tranmere a £25,000 'facility fee' to get him on loan until the end of the season, Tony Butler, for £140,000, from Port Vale reserves, Neil Clement, on loan from Chelsea until the end of the season and, last but not least, to the surprise of the Albion faithful – Bob Taylor.

It turned out that discussions had been going on for some time. Bob, who had not moved from his Lichfield home, had been told by Bolton that he was now surplus to requirements, and would be released at the end of the season. Even so, there was still a tremendous incentive to remain at the Reebok, and fight for his place, for Bolton were still in the promotion race, and had reached the semi-final of the FA Cup, and were soon to play Aston Villa at Wembley. However, the pull of a return to his spiritual home was too great, and Bob jumped at the move. The local press gave news of the deal. "Taylor will end his playing days at The Hawthorns after agreeing a three year deal. While his arrival will be welcomed by his many fans, it represents a last throw of the dice by desperate Albion. They have been forced to fork out a fee believed to be £100,000 to bring back Taylor, who was allowed to leave for nothing by former boss Denis Smith. Megson hopes that Taylor can add some much-needed firepower to the team."

The signing gave the players and the fans a lift, and Andy Townsend was quick to welcome Bob. "New faces are always going to freshen things up a bit and lift everyone – Bob was obviously a big favourite and hero last time here and hopefully he can come in and produce the sort of form that he showed last time round."

Lee Hughes, for one, was looking forward to playing with Bob. "He is still a fans' favourite and his arrival has given the dressing room a big boost. He's a different style of striker to me, but I'm sure we can bring the best out of each other. We didn't start many games together during his first spell here, but he's someone I have always looked up to and respected. He's like a mentor."

When Taylor signed, it was also announced that he would be granted a Testimonial – to make up for the loss of wages that he was taking to leave the former Premiership side. Effectively, he would be earning two thirds of his salary at the Reebok, so a Testimonial – a surefire thing at the Albion for a player of Bob's popularity – would enable the fans to show their appreciation of Bob's efforts at the club. But May 2003 was a long way away; there was still a lot of work to do.

Bob's 'Second Coming' came against third in the League Manchester City at Maine Road. City, in front of a full house 32,000 crowd, baying for promotion, were never easy opponents for Albion at the best of times. This time Megson threw in all his new players – including Des Lyttle, his other pre-deadline signing – to give debuts to no less than five new men, the greatest number of debutants for an Albion game since the Second World War. And they gave a superb performance. Despite some heavy pressure from the home side, the game was goalless at the break. In the 59th minute Lee Hughes shocked the huge crowd when he curled a right foot shot into the top corner of the net, past Weaver, to give Albion a deserved lead.

Mark Kennedy equalised for the Blues eighteen minutes later, when

Up-close and personal —Bob means business back in the blue and white stripes

Albion fell asleep at a free kick, and Bob's 'second debut' was ruined, in injury time, when a left wing cross from Dickov was deflected into the path of Goater, who side-footed past Brian Jensen from eight yards. That there was to be no immediate 'fairy-tale' return for Bob was confirmed when Walsall's result at Tranmere came through. They had drawn 1-1, and Albion slipped down into the bottom three.

Bob's return to his old stamping ground came in the next match, when Albion took on Ipswich Town – another side looking for automatic promotion – at The Hawthorns. Bob, of course, got a wonderful welcome from his old fans, who were looking for his partnership with a new favourite, Lee Hughes, to be the cornerstone of an Albion revival. Sadly, it was not to be; Bob's striking partnership with Lee was destined to last for all of 43 minutes. That was how long it took for the youngster to score the opening goal – and, in the process, get clattered by goalkeeper Richard Wright.

Hughes limped painfully off the field and although, at first, the club insisted the injury was not a serious one, it turned out that he had broken a bone in his knee, and would not play again that season, Suddenly, and dramatically, the responsibility of scoring the goals to keep Albion up had fallen squarely on the broad shoulders of Bob Taylor. "When we lost Hughesie, everybody thought that that meant it was all over – that we were going down then. But actually, I thought we did better after that. No disrespect to Hughesie, but we went on from there, and hardly lost a game, even though we were drawing a few. We did get stronger, we didn't cave in. And a lot of that was down to the manager, making us tighter."

There was no respite on the field. Four days after the draw with Ipswich, Albion had to take on another side battling for promotion, Barnsley – the First Division's top scorers – at Oakwell. After another goalless first half, Albion took the lead in the 47th minute when Fabian De Freitas was brought down in the box, and his compatriot Richard Sneekes converted the penalty. The lead lasted all of five minutes, when Bernard equalised, but four minutes after that came the goal that all Albion fans had been waiting for. Jason van Blerk launched a free kick into the box, and Taylor met it on the full, looping a brilliant header over and across Kevin Miller, to put Albion ahead for a second time. "My first goal back at Barnsley meant a lot to me. There were great expectations about me coming back, and I didn't want to spoil the previous six and a half years at the club, so I was worried about what would happen." But, for the second Saturday in a row, Albion threw points away, allowing Neil Shipperley to score a last minute equaliser for the Tykes.

If that was high drama – it was nothing compared to the next game, when Bolton Wanderers, of all clubs, arrived at The Hawthorns desperate for points to reach the Play-offs. The match turned out to be a rollercoaster of a game that few fans will ever forget. There was certainly plenty of 'edge' to the game, with, apart from Bob, two other ex-Trotters in the Albion side, in De Freitas and Sneekes, and it was the two Dutchmen who combined to give Albion the opening goal. As at Barnsley, De Freitas was fouled in the area, and Sneekes scored from the penalty spot, in the 22nd minute. Bolton levelled through Hansen fourteen minutes later, but by the break Albion were ahead again thanks to a diving header from the battling Sean Flynn.

Ten minutes into the second half Bergsson brought Bolton level for a second time and then, in the 66th minute, the visitors stunned the home fans by taking the lead, through Gudjohnson. Back came Albion, with the goal of the game in the 80th minute — and it was SuperBob who scored it, against his former colleagues. A sweeping move saw Quinn feed Potter on the right; his high cross seemed to be going out, but Santos met it, and headed the ball back across the box for Taylor to net with a brilliant overhead kick that left Jaskelainen helpless as it dropped over him, into the top corner.

With the crowd in a frenzy, Albion broke away with two minutes left, when Sneekes raced down the pitch before sidefooting a pass to young Adam Oliver, who met the ball first time to lift it high into a gaping net. It seemed as if the 18-year old had scored the goal that might

Bob celebrates the first goal of his second spell at the Albion, at Barnsley

effectively keep Albion in the First Division – but for the third week running Albion blew it, when Bergsson scored another equaliser to make it 4-4 in the last minute. "Of all the teams to play against, we had Bolton. What a game, it was just like when I came down to the Albion the season before. Going ahead, going behind, going ahead again, and then ending up as 4-4. Incredible. When they went 3-2 up, I felt I was fouled by Gudni Bergsson, but he put it in, and it was down to me for giving the ball away. Then we get away to the other end, and I score an overhead kick – tremendous!

But if those dropped points were bad, worse was to follow. On Easter Saturday Albion met Walsall in a six-pointer at the Bescot Stadium, and turned in an inept performance. Bob had his poorest game since his return as Albion lost an early lead to lose to a Tom Bennett goal eight minutes from time. Once again, Walsall leapfrogged the Baggies, to drop Bob's side into the bottom three once more, a point adrift of safety.

Easter Monday – what better day for Bob to fully resurrect his Albion career. And what better opposition, in the form of Alan Buckley's Grimsby Town, who arrived at The Hawthorns for a game that Albion had to win. The Mariners had no less than five former colleagues of Bob's in their side; Stacey Coldicott, Paul Groves, Dave Smith, Lee Ashcroft and Kevin Donovan.

For SuperBob, the game was a milestone in his career, as Albion won 2-1, and Bob scored both the goals. The first came after fifteen minutes, a diving header from a Sneekes' cross. His second came two minutes into the second half, when he pounced on a loose ball in the box, poking it home past Danny Coyne. Fittingly, it came at the Birmingham Road End, and it turned out to be his one hundredth League goal for the Albion. On the same afternoon, Walsall lost to West Midlands opposition for the first time that season, going down 2-1 to Blues at St Andrews, allowing Albion to move two points clear of the Saddlers. After the Grimsby game, Gary Megson paid tribute to his centre-forward. "Bob has been a credit to himself. There were a few eyebrows raised when we gave him a long contract to bring him back; but we knew just how important he would be. You see how the crowd react to him. His goals have been invaluable to us, not to mention his experience and knowledge of the game."

The season was building up to an unbearable climax, but there was a pleasant interlude for the players and fans after the Grimsby win, when the Supporters Club held its *Player of The Year* Night at the Tower Ballroom in Edgbaston. There was a pleasant surprise for Bob too. Supporters Club chairman Dave Holloway called him up to present the *Goal of The Season* Award, and Bob's face was a picture when he opened up the envelope to announce the result, only to find that HE had won it for his fabulous overhead kick against Bolton!

On the penultimate weekend of the season, Albion battled out a nervy goalless draw against QPR. The supporters had their end of season jamboree at Loftus Road, dressing up in suits, ties and dark glasses in response to a survey which had declared that Albion's fans were the worst-dressed in the League. The solitary point was better than nothing, but with Walsall beating Portsmouth 1-0 it meant that the two clubs went into the last Sunday of the season level on 46 points, but with Albion marginally ahead on goal difference. Although it appeared that Albion and Walsall were both fighting for the last available safe spot, both clubs could be saved if Crewe – on 45 points – lost their last match and both Black Country sides won.

On the final day, Walsall had the misfortune to be at in-form Ipswich, Crewe were at Barnsley, whilst Albion had home advantage over already-promoted First Division champions, Charlton Athletic. For the second time in his Albion career Bob went into the last game of the season knowing that he had to help Albion to a win to ensure First Division survival. Facing him were the Addicks, and his old striking partner Andy Hunt, returning to The Hawthorns for the first time since leaving the Baggies. In a pre-match interview, Hunt recalled his old partnership with Bob. "He was brilliant to play alongside. We probably played about eighty games together, and I remember that we always seemed to have a good record; one of us tended to score in most games. Bob is a lot bigger and stronger than I am, but we seemed to complement each other. People say that you shouldn't go back to your former clubs, but with Bob it was different; I don't think Bob wanted to leave in the first place. I really hope Albion stay up and the game is played in a party atmosphere."

And so it was – but only after a tense first half in which Albion fans learned that Crewe were winning at Barnsley, and Walsall were doing well to hold out at Portman Road. Albion's luck began to turn after 49 minutes, when news came through that Albion fan David Johnson had put Ipswich ahead against Walsall.

In the 1995-96 season Sneekes and Taylor had helped keep Albion in Division One with an end-of-season goal flurry. In the bright Hawthorns sunshine in 2000, the two combined to put Albion ahead in the 65th minute, when Sneekes sidestepped Carl Tiler to shoot past Dean Kiely. Even with Albion a goal up, there was still plenty of tension in the air, as Charlton maintained their efforts to end on a winning note – although it was quite clear that Andy Hunt had no intention of spoiling the party. "I spoke to Andy Hunt before the game, of course, a quick word. He had one effort that was cleared off the line; that was close. But we still had to score the goals. Richard's was a good goal, and mine was like the one at Barnsley, but it wasn't as if the goals were given to us. So we stopped up; a great finish to the season."

Albion needed a second goal to ensure that they could not be upset by a late Walsall comeback – and it came in the 70th minute. And, to use an old cliché, it could not have been better scripted. Neil Clement went on a powerful left wing run to reach the byeline, and cross strongly into the penalty area. At the far post was SuperBob, and he dispatched a great header into the far corner of the net, for his fifth goal in eight games since returning home.

Ten minutes later, the party really began when news filtered through of Ipswich's second goal against Walsall; at the final whistle, the Albion fans invaded the pitch, to revel in the sun, secure in the knowledge that their side was safe for another year.

Bob was well and truly back home. As Gary Megson conceded, "Bob Taylor has now scored five goals in eight games. He has done everything I asked of him – and more!" But there was still plenty of action left for SuperBob at The Hawthorns.

Richard Sneekes and Bob celebrate after the second goal against Charlton

The Baggies and the Play-offs

After their last day survival routine against Charlton, Albion looked to strengthen the side — Gary Megson was endeavouring to build a side that could perhaps challenge for a Play-off place. For the second year running the Baggies toured Denmark in pre-season, playing three games against Naestved, FC Copenhagen (managed by Roy Hodgson) and Greve, their 'nursery' side. Bob figured in every game, and got off the mark with one of the four goals against part-timers Greve.

Back in England, India paid a visit to The Hawthorns, and forced a goalless draw in a sterile game that was broadcast back live to the sub-continent. Then it was off to Meadow Lane, where Albion beat newly promoted Notts County 3-0, and Bob collected two more goals. The game was more significant in that it marked the arrival of Jason Roberts. Albion had been chasing the player – the nephew of former Albion 'Great' Cyrille Regis — for some time, and finally paid out £2m to Bristol Rovers to bring the prolific striker to The Hawthorns. It meant fresh competition up front for Bob – or, alternatively, a new striking partner. Megson experimented with a front three of Hughes, Taylor and Roberts in the next friendly, Roberts marking his full debut with the equaliser in a

Bob in action in an unusual pre-season friendly against the Indian national side

115

disappointing 1-1 draw at home to Second Division Swindon Town.

Megson persisted with his three strikers for the last warm-up game, at Saltergate, but Third Division Chesterfield, managed by ex-Baggie Ian Banks embarrassed the Baggies by winning 1-0. Between them, Taylor, Hughes and Roberts contrived to miss a boatload of chances.

After a month of preparation, Albion kicked off the new season on August 12, with a tough away trip at recently relegated Nottingham Forest. New signing Derek McInnes made his debut in midfield, but Bob started on the bench, as Megson went with Hughes and Roberts in attack. Bob replaced James Quinn after 65 minutes, but the whole side drew a blank, as they went down to a 77th minute goal from Jon Olaf Hjelde – who should have been sent off in the first half for a professional foul on Roberts.

Four days later, Bob was turning out for the Reserves at Vale Park. Nothing unusual about that – but worth recording because he scored a superb goal, technically one of the best of his career. The game was seventeen minutes old when Bob met a poor clearance from Delaney in the Valiant's goal. He controlled the ball with his left foot, before volleying home from 25 yards out, with the goalkeeper stranded; a magnificent goal, and the only one of the game.

Bob was still on the subs' bench for the next game, a 2-0 home defeat by Sam Allardyce's Bolton Wanderers, and did not get his

Bob scores — as usual — against the Blues, in a 1-1 draw at The Hawthorns

116

first 'start' of the season until the side travelled to the Vetch and forced a goalless draw with Swansea in the Worthington Cup. He kept his place for the trip to Barnsley the following Saturday, when the Tykes made it three League defeats on the trot for the Albion. That 4-1 defeat was the turning point of the Albion's season. Despite failing to score – Lee Hughes had scored the club's first goal of the season – Bob kept his place for the next five games, as Albion were unbeaten, with wins against QPR, Crystal Palace and Swansea. On September 17, Bob scored his first League goal of the season, in the home game against old favourites, Blues.

Albion had had a poor recent record against Birmingham, but two minutes into the game SuperBob ran onto a Jason van Blerk pass, rode two tackles and blasted the ball past Ian Bennett. Unfortunately, it was not enough to provide Albion with their first win against their neighbours in five games; Bob was substituted in the 63rd minute, and twelve minutes later Geoff Horsfield equalised.

Bob got his reward for his goal – he was dropped, and did not start a game again until November 4! In that time, Albion played ten games, and lost three, at home to Derby in the Cup, at home to Norwich, and away to Grimsby. At Blundell Park, Albion totally dominated the first half, but with Jason Roberts wasting several

Bob heads a goal back for Albion against Derby in the FA Cup at Pride Park

opportunities, just could not score. The home side re-thought their tactics in the second half – Albion didn't, and lost 2-0. Bob played the last twelve minutes of the game, but by then it was much too late.

Lee Hughes was suspended for the home game against Burnley on November 4, so Bob was restored to the starting line-up. He did not have a particularly good game, looking short of match fitness, and the rest of the side played badly against a rough and tumble Burnley outfit. The Clarets led from the 23rd minute, but three minutes from time Taylor made his one telling contribution to the game, moving onto a pass from Quinn and crossing low and hard for Jason Roberts to steer the ball past ex-Baggie Paul Crichton. As the season unfolded, Bob's contribution in both games against Burnley would turn out to be absolutely vital.

Bob was back on the bench for the away game at Huddersfield the following week, as Hughes returned to the side; the Hughes-Roberts partnership was beginning to click, and Albion lost just one of their next five games, at home to runaway leaders Fulham.

One great game that Bob did feature in – albeit for only three minutes – was the epic 3-3 draw against Watford at Vicarage Road. With Tony Butler hammering in a classic own goal, Albion had gone two goals down, only to turn on the style, and go 3-2 up. In the 80th minute, Butler erred once more, to present Tommy Mooney with an equaliser. Enter SuperBob; he came on in the 87th minute; in the dying seconds of the game, he delivered the perfect cushioned header for Richard Sneekes, six yards out and unmarked. Sneekes, with one eye on the ball, and another on goalkeeper Baardsen, missed the ball completely...

At the halfway stage of the season, Albion were fourth in the table, with 41 points from 23 games. That left them two points behind Blues, four behind Bolton and an unbridgeable fourteen points adrift of leaders Fulham. For Bob it was a bitter-sweet sensation – he was happy to see Albion in a Play-off position, but in those 23 games he had only had six starts, and his goal tally – still just the one against Blues – made it the worst season so far in his career, in purely goalscoring terms.

In the FA Cup Albion drew Premiership Derby County away – a repeat of the earlier meeting between the sides in the Worthington Cup. Bob – as he would be for the next five games – was substitute, and he watched in horror as Derby raced into a 3-0 lead. Bob came on in the 72nd minute, and Albion bossed the rest of the game, with Roberts on the left wing and Bob up front with Hughes.

Four minutes after getting on, Bob headed home a simple chance after a run and cross from Roberts. Three minutes after that, Hughes wrong-footed keeper Matt Poom with a neat backheader from a Ruel Fox cross, but despite a spirited charge, ably led by Bob, Albion could not force an equaliser.

During the season, Bob had been writing a weekly column in the *Sports Argus*, mostly on the day-to-day trivia that happens at every football club. After the Derby game he found a few words to bemoan his own season so far. "I managed to get the first of our goals on Saturday and it was nice to get on the scoresheet again. But it was only my second strike of the season – and that's an absolute disgrace as far as I am concerned. I've had the odd chance when I've come off the bench, but whether it's been down to the woodwork, the goalkeeper or my own poor finishing, they haven't been going in. In an ideal world I would have scored more goals, but that's just a fantasy. With Hughesie and Roberts playing so well, all I can do is bide my time"

And bide his time he did. During January Bob had the meagre consolation of a goal for the Reserves in a 2-0 win at Barnsley, and it was February 20 before he came off the bench to take his place in the starting line-up against Crewe at The Hawthorns. Bob celebrated in the best possible fashion, with a cracking goal. In the 23rd minute Sneekes found Ruel Fox, and when the little winger

Bob's on the deck, but he's scored against Crewe in a 2-2 draw

whipped over a cross, Bob, with his back to goal, swivelled to meet the ball first time, on the volley, and smashed it home past Bankole from twelve yards. The game ended 2-2, but Bob's return to the side was brief. He played in the next two games, a 2-0 home win over Portsmouth — Russell Hoult's debut game – and a sterile 1-0 defeat at Blackburn, before being handed the sub's jersey once again.

On March 18, Bob was not even in the squad, as the team turned in one of its worst performances of the season. What was really unfortunate was that they chose Molineux as the venue for such a lack-lustre showing. The Baggies were short on both effort and quality, as they went down 3-1. Jason Roberts, in particular, had a hard time against his old club, and Albion slipped down to sixth place in the table. With only one win in nine games they were in danger of missing out on a Play-off spot. Who better to help steady the ship than SuperBob?

He was recalled for the game against Tranmere the following week, and, looking more like his old self, he responded with both goals in a 2-1 home win. The first, on 39 minutes, was lashed in off the post after Sneekes had set him up. The second, 23 minutes later, though, was vintage Bob. Tranmere centre-half Graham Allen was trying to shepherd a long ball back to his goalkeeper, but Bob muscled past him and then used his strength to hold off his opponent as he lobbed the ball over the advancing Achterberg.

Bob scores against Tranmere, despite the attention of Sean Flynn and Mickey Mellon

Jason Koumas pulled a goal back for doomed Tranmere at the death, but Albion held on for all three points – and Bob had doubled his goal tally for the season.

That brace of goals took a weight off Bob's shoulders – and set him up for his most important goal of the season. On April 14 Albion travelled to Turf Moor – never the most hospitable of places – to take on one of the form sides just below them in the table. Glen Little put Burnley ahead early in the second half, and then the home side battered Albion, who, for long periods, just could not get the ball out of their own half. Defeat was unthinkable, for it would have handed Burnley a lifeline which would almost certainly have seen them overtake the Baggies for the final Play-off spot. When all seemed lost, up popped Bob to head home a centre from Ruel Fox. There were just two minutes left on the clock, and the travelling Albion fans could not believe their good fortune. At the end of the season the true significance of that goal became apparent – as Albion finished in sixth place, just two points ahead of Burnley.

Bob's most important goal of the season turned out to be his last of the campaign. He played in the next two games, a shock 1-0 defeat

Nostalgia time for Bob, as he lines up in a '93 XI' side for the 2001 Daryl Burgess Testimonial, alongside Lilwall, Reid, Hunt, Garner, Bradley, Hamilton and Co.

at home to Grimsby, and a 2-1 win at Gillingham, but was left out of the last home game, against Huddersfield, as Albion booked a place in the Play-offs against, of all clubs, Bolton Wanderers. In the build-up the semi-final encounter, there was naturally a great deal of attention focused on both Bob and Richard Sneekes, both of whom had enjoyed happy times at the Reebok. For Bolton manager Sam Allardyce it was a chance of sweet revenge. Dudley-born Sam had had a spell as assistant manager at The Hawthorns under Brian Talbot, and had been very bitter about his sacking in 1991.

Bob was looking forward to the clash. He had played for Bolton at Wembley in the Play-off Final of 1999, when they had lost to Watford, and had much to be grateful for at the Lancashire side. "I came back to Albion feeling like a new player in many ways, and that's all down to the experiences I had at Bolton. Having said that, I won't have any problem about scoring against them, should the chances come my way."

Despite the possibility of using Bob's motivation to score against his old side, Megson went with Jason Roberts for the first leg of the semi-final at The Hawthorns. Bob, as he had been for thirty games already, was named as substitute.

Everything looked rosy when first Jason Roberts, then Lee Hughes, from the penalty spot, gave Albion a two goal lead; the sun was shining and the capacity Hawthorns crowd was boinging. Even when, with ten minutes left, Gudni Bergsson pulled a goal back, it looked as if Albion would be taking a vital lead to the second leg at the Reebok. Megson brought on fresh legs – Bob and Adam Chambers – to hold onto the lead, but three minutes from time Bo Hansen skipped into the box, Phil Gilchrist challenged – and Per Frandsen converted the penalty.

For Albion, the second leg was a non-event in football terms. Bolton ran the game from the start – or almost from the start, after Jason Roberts had put a great chance into the side-netting. After that the home side had it all their own way, and ran home easy 3-0 winners. Bob came on for the last 26 minutes, but by then the tie was long lost, and it would be no happy return to the Reebok. In spite of the nature of the defeat, the Albion fans remained long after the final whistle to celebrate the considerable achievements of a side that, twelve months earlier, looked certainties for the Second Division.

Sadly, the game turned out to be the last appearance in an Albion shirt for another ex-Trotter, Richard Sneekes, who was released a couple of days later. For Bob, though, in many ways, the best was yet to come.

Back to the Premiership

At the start of the 2001-02 season, Bob was back, with the rest of the Albion squad, in beautiful downtown Copenhagen, where the club had arranged another series of four friendlies against local sides. He got on the scoresheet in two of the games, against Greve and Slagelse – and found he had a new strike partner, as Megson had signed young Scott Dobie from Carlisle United, a raw and inexperienced winger who was surely an investment for the future.

Albion's problems really started once they were back in England, and playing warm-up games there. On July 25 Jason Roberts broke a bone in his foot in a 2-1 win at Cheltenham, reducing Albion's strike force by one. Then, in the week following the Sunderland friendly, just as the Nationwide League season was about to begin, Lee Hughes was sold to Coventry City for the odd amount of one pound over five million. He had a clause in his contract that he could leave the club if anyone tabled a bid over £5m, so on Wednesday August 8 he moved to Highfield Road. Hughes' parting shot to the Albion was that he thought that Coventry, just relegated from the Premiership, were a better bet than Albion for a return to the top flight. With the season fast approaching, Megson was left with a strike force consisting of a novice – Scott Dobie – and a 'veteran' – SuperBob! Bob was sanguine about his stroke of luck. "If Lee had stopped at the Albion, and Jason Roberts hadn't got injured, I don't think I would have played much last season. I would have just played a bit part; a lot like this season, I think. But I've got different attributes to them. It's not about pace, it's about holding the ball up, bringing people into play – and scoring goals."

Bob on tour, in Aabenra, Denmark. Back row, left to right: Appleton, Clement, Roberts, Butler, Adamson, Bob, Sigurdsson. Front: Fox, McInnes, Gilchrist, Lyttle

On the opening day of the season, Hughes scored on his debut as the Sky Blues won at Stockport. At the same time Albion were at Bescot playing Walsall, who had made a quick return to the First Division. The Saddlers had no problem in beating an ineffectual Albion side, for whom Dobie and Taylor drew a blank.

When Grimsby came to The Hawthorns the Baggies were expected to get back on track quickly, especially when two minutes into the second half, Scott Dobie was fouled in the box, and referee Scott Mathieson gave a penalty.

With Albion's spot kick expert playing for Coventry, it was Bob who grabbed the ball and placed it on the penalty spot. It was his first penalty kick for six years, and he placed his effort too close to Coyne, who beat the ball away — and then recovered his ground to brilliantly save Ruel Fox's follow-up. "I think I started a trend! One that unfortunately stayed with us for the rest of the season, right up to the Bradford game. It was no spur of the moment thing; in the dressing room before the game, the gaffer had asked me if I wanted to be 'on penalties.' And I said, 'Yeah, definitely.' Lo and behold we got one, and it was down to me to take it. And what can I say? I missed. Well, I hit the target, at least – but he saved it! You know, you should always score from twelve yards. Especially as a striker. You know, if you get those sort of chances in a game, you put them away nine times out of ten."

Bob was replaced by James Quinn in the 76th minute, and thirty seconds later Larus Sigurdsson conceded a penalty at the other end, for Pouton to convert and give the Mariners a shock win.

Bob kept his place for the midweek trip to the Abbey Stadium, for the Worthington Cup game at Cambridge, a one-off tie that had to be settled on the night. Scott Dobie gave Albion an early lead, only for

Bob's last penalty for the Albion — saved by Grimsby's Danny Coyne

Alcide to equalise for the home side, with eleven minutes left – after Cambridge had had a goal disallowed because there were two balls on the pitch! The match was still level after ninety minutes, when Bob was once more substituted by Quinn, and with no further scoring in extra time, Albion won 4-3 on penalties. In the light of what was to come, it was indeed ironic that, in their first test of the season, penalty takers Quinn, Balis, Appleton and Clement all put away their kicks with consummate ease!

Megson appreciated that Albion were desperately short of forward cover, so he went out and signed Daniel Dichio on loan from Sunderland. It was Bob who gave way to the lanky striker, at Sheffield Wednesday, when Dichio made an immediate impact, scoring Albion's goal in a 1-1 draw – and following that up with the winner a week later in the 1-0 home win against Gillingham.

Bob was facing the prospect of moving even further down the strikers' pecking order a week later, when Jason Roberts was pronounced fit again, and lined up alongside Dichio for the home game against promotion favourites Manchester City at The Hawthorns; both Bob and Scott Dobie were relegated to the bench. The Baggies got off to a great start, when captain Derek McInnes scored a super volley after just ten minutes. Five minutes into the second half, though, Roberts limped off, to be replaced by Dobie; the Grenadian striker had broken the same bone in his foot, and the injury would keep him out of the side until December.

Clement put Albion two goals up with a penalty in the 66th minute. Two minutes later Dichio had to go off with a bad ankle injury that prematurely ended his loan spell, and Bob came on. In the 79th minute it was Bob who was upended twenty five yards out, and Clement scored a wonderful goal from the free kick. Scott Dobie rounded off a resounding result with his first Albion League goal seven minutes from time.

The double injury blow to Roberts and Dichio meant that Megson was back to square one, and forced to rely on the Taylor-Dobie partnership – which served the club well.

Bob missed just one of the next thirteen games. At Watford he set up the opening goal for Dobie when he cushioned a headed pass into the youngster's path. In the second half Taylor launched himself into the box with a determined dribble, only to be fouled by Galli. Dobie took the penalty, which was saved by Baardsen, but the keeper failed to hold onto the ball, and Dobie followed up to score. In the melee that followed twenty players were involved in a scuffle which ended with Galli and Bob both booked – and later led to a £20,000 fine for Watford. In the end it took a last minute penalty save from Russell Hoult to win the game for Albion, after Tony Butler had been sent off.

Wins against Preston, Portsmouth and Burnley followed, along with home defeats by Wimbledon and Millwall. Bob was playing well, but, much to his chagrin, he couldn't find the net. The breakthrough came on October 16 when he scored twice at Stockport. County had both Richard Sneekes and Jason van Blerk in their side, although neither played very well. "We were told before that game about the two ex-Albion lads in the County side, Richard Sneekes and Jason van Blerk; 'Don't go talking to them, leave them alone.' But I played with Richard a long while, and I think he's a good lad, and I don't see why I shouldn't talk to somebody. But yes, Richard was quiet throughout the game, but I don't know whether that was down to us, or because of his mood at the time, or what. I tangled with van Blerk though. We had a bit of a go at each other after he elbowed me in the face. I told him what I thought of him at the time, and that was that!"

Bob opened the scoring in the ninth minute, when he scored with a left-footed volley from fifteen yards. "It was great to get the goals, but it was more important to get the win, which we really needed at the time. It's the same for Lee this season. He's been unlucky this year. He just needs a goal to take the burden off him, and then he'll start scoring. The fans want you to score and it's a relief for them as well. And one you've got one, you always think that it might be the chance for you to go off on a scoring frenzy – scoring five or six goals. And that's what you're judged on as a striker. Goals! Not your all-round play, which is what it should be, but goals, pure and simple."

On the hour mark, Bob smashed home a close range shot after the keeper had pushed out Clement's header, and Albion ran out fairly comfortable winners against the worst side in the division. After the game, Megson praised Taylor's efforts, whilst stressing the need for more cover. "Bob's first goal was a great finish – and his second was just what we wanted. He did very well, but that doesn't change the fact that we do need to bring in another striker. If Taylor or Dobie had been injured, I would have been scratching around to find somebody."

In *The Baggies* newspaper Michael Appleton also commended his team mate. "It was great to see Bob score, but I have to say that they were two angry goals. The first was a great one. I think he tried to bust the net with it; you could see that there was a lot of frustration being unleashed. It had all the hallmarks of a striker who hasn't scored for a while. It will do wonders for his confidence."

Just when things were picking up nicely, Bob got himself sent off at Barnsley. Albion have always had a poor record at Oakwell, and the game on October 28 did nothing to change it. new signing Andy Johnson scored with a marvellous long range lob after just ten minutes, but Bruce Dyer equalised straight away, and Sigurdsson gave away a blatant penalty for Lumsden to put the home side ahead.

Two minutes from time Dyer seemed to have sealed the game, but in the final seconds Clement smashed home a great free kick to make it 3-2. "I ran into the net to get the ball. As I picked it up, the keeper grabbed it off me, holding it close, and I tried to grab it back. He pushed against me, face to face, and I stood up and pushed my face into his. I didn't head butt him, I just pushed my head into his face, like pushing noses together. The referee said that I head-butted him – but if I had, I think he would have gone down. I didn't – but I wish I had now! It was stupid, but it wasn't malicious – I was just trying to get the ball back. I didn't realise that it was the same keeper that had fouled me and got sent off at Exeter back in 1993, not until I was told about it afterwards. I don't really hold grudges like that anyway – but after that I couldn't wait until he came to The Hawthorns! I was waiting for him, but I never got the chance. And I don't know whether I would have done anything anyway…"

Little did he know it – but Bob was the hundredth Albion player to be sent off in the 124-year history of the club. The end result for Bob's third dismissal of his career was a club fine of two weeks' wages, and a three match ban.

Albion had been chasing another loan striker to shore up their depleted forward line, and Bob's impending suspension made that all the more essential. In came former German international Uwe Rosler, from Southampton. He made his debut alongside Bob at Crystal Palace on October 31, and went close to a debut goal when he headed against the bar in the first half. In the 63rd minute Russell Hoult launched a huge clearance downfield.

Bob's third sending off — Albion's 100th!

127

"That was typical Wimbledon tactics. A big boot down the field from Russell, over a defender, and I got my body in the way of two defenders, and rolled them. Fortunately for me, I rolled towards the six yard box, and as the keeper came out, I just knocked it past him. Kolinko; that must have cost me an extra fiver at the end of the season!"

Bob's last game before his suspension was at home to Nottingham Forest – 1-0 to the Albion – with Rosler scoring the goal. By the time Bob was available again, the German had returned to Southampton in a fit of pique – but Danny Dichio had signed from Sunderland for £1.25m. The upshot of that was that Bob made just one start in the next twenty nine League and Cup games. That was at Crewe on December 15, the night that Jason Roberts made his second comeback of the season when he replaced Bob in the 68th minute.

With Bob firmly on the bench, and making the odd appearance late in games, the side climbed steadily up the table and reached the quarter-finals of the FA Cup, where they lost 1-0 at home to Fulham. The defining moment of the season – for Albion and for Bob, in particular – came at Deepdale on February 26. Albion lost 1-0 to Preston, Neil Clement missed a penalty, and, just before half time, Jason Roberts broke his foot for the third time. This time he was out for the rest of the season, and most Albion fans leaving the ground that night thought that any chance of automatic promotion had gone. Their side was third in the table, only two points behind Manchester City, but a massive ten points adrift of leaders Wolves.

Danny Dichio put Albion back on the winning track with the only goal at Wimbledon, then rescued a point in a 1-1 draw at home to Watford.

Bob looks on in disbelief as Mr Wolstenholme gets the red card out again

Then, on March 16, came the Battle of Bramall Lane. "I think that was one of those days that you will never forget. Not just because of what happened on the pitch, but everything else that happened that day. I mean, I was sub, and I was warming up and I was getting pelted from the main stand. I think it was because they knew I was originally with Leeds – that was part of it – but also there was a time when I had a chance to join Sheffield United, and turned them down. I was warming up, and I can remember this guy running across the corner of the pitch, with a West Brom flag, and we realised that he was a United fan, who'd pinched the flag, so all that kicked off. Then the stewards behind us kept moaning because we were blocking their view. What did they want us to do? We were doing our stretches – and trying to do our job – and they wanted us to move. So all that was starting."

Bob did not enter the fray until the 56th minute, when he replaced Adam Chambers. By that time Albion were leading through Dobie's 18th minute header, but Simon Tracey, the home goalkeeper, had already been sent off. Five minutes after Bob's arrival, McInnes made it 2-0 with Albion's Goal of The Season. "Then everything kicked off. I saw the Santos tackle, but I saw it from behind. It was awful — but did-n't think it was a bad tackle at the time, because of the angle I was at. Then I saw the best head-butt I have ever seen! Suffo on Derek McInnes. It was sweet; no noise, just bang, and he was down. Sweet as a pea, blood everywhere. Then I can remember somebody shouting for people to go down – and to get sent off. I told the referee that their number seven was walking off the pitch. He said, 'No, no, it's OK.' But I told him again, and he said, 'No, my assistant has sorted that out.' But he hadn't — he was leaving the pitch without permission. Then one of their players was telling his team mates to try to get sent off – and so, for a spell of five minutes, every time the ball came towards Dobes, or one of our strikers, Curle was trying to do them, and there was a lot of face-to-face confrontation. At the end, because nobody was getting sent off, they told the left back to go down. They knew what they were doing. They knew exactly what they were doing."

Dobie put Albion three up, and the points looked secure. Bizarrely, it would be another five days before Albion would be awarded the three points. First Michael Brown slipped quietly off the field. Then, in the 82nd minute, Rob Ullathorpe went down with a 'muscle spasm' and United were reduced to six men, and the referee, Eddie Wolstenholme, had no option other than to abandon the match. FIFA had introduced a ruling that stated that a match could not continue if one side had less than seven men on the pitch, but this was the first time that the ruling had been applied in a match in England. A meeting of the Football

League Management Committee on the following Thursday awarded the Albion – who had kept their heads in the face of extreme provocation — the points, but it had been the most extraordinary game of football that Bob had ever been involved in.

"Now, I knew Georges Santos from his loan spell at the Albion. And he was a great lad. But now you're talking retribution, and that's a personal thing. At the end of the day Georges had his cheek bone and his eye socket broken, and he could have lost the sight of his eye. You're touching personal things now; you're only human, and you want your revenge. I think that's the way it was. It had nothing to do with football, or Sheffield United against West Bromwich Albion. It was Andy Johnson and Georges Santos. You could have taken them off and put them outside, and it would still have gone off…"

After the drama and the controversy of Bramall Lane, the next game, against Nottingham Forest was quite a tame affair. Bob was still on the bench, as the manager persevered with the Dichio-Dobie combination, but he replaced Dichio after an hour's play. The match was heading for goalless stalemate until eight minutes from time. Ricardo Scimeca needlessly fouled Scott Dobie, 25 yards from goal. "I came on and scored the goal. I was in the box for the free kick, shouting at Clem to give me the ball so I could get a quick shot in on goal. But they were calming it down, so I moved to the side of the wall. Now, I've always been told that as they take the free kick, you push yourself into the wall, to give the taker more room to bend it around; but as you do that, spin out to pick up any rebounds. And that's what I did. Just what you're taught, just like riding a bike – something you learn and you remember,

Bob the joker, pre-season 2001-02. Back row, Nick Worth, A Chambers, Dobie, J Chambers, Balis, Bob (with wig), Sigurdsson, Dave Matthews. Middle: Ade Stovell, Jordao, Hughes, Appleton, Adamson, Hoult, Quinn, Gilchrist, Butler, Gary Sheton. Front: Oliver, Fox, McInnes, Frank Burrows, Gary Megson, Lyttle, Clement, Cummings, Roberts

that you do instinctively." It was Bob's fourth goal of the season – all on opposition territory, and responsible for winning nine valuable points for the Baggies. The gap between Albion and Wolves was now five points – and Albion had a goal in hand.

Gary Megson appreciated that the win was down to Bob's experience. "If Bob's got anything, it's the instincts of a forward. I'm not sure anybody would have followed up the free kick in the manner Bob did, if he hadn't been on the field. His goal looked dead easy but it was all down to his anticipation of where the ball might drop."

The next day Wolves stuttered to a goalless draw with Norwich at Molineux; it was their fourth game without a win, and the pressure was beginning to tell. The following Wednesday Bob played the last fifteen minutes of the game against Crewe, but the game had already been won, for Albion were already 4-1 up when Bob come off the bench. The gap at the top was now three points, with both Black Country clubs having played 41 games.

As Easter, and the transfer deadline approached, Albion signed Stanislav Varga on loan from Sunderland, and striker Trevor Benjamin from Leicester. Three short weeks ago, automatic promotion seemed a fantasy – now, with Wolves all over the place, it was beginning to dawn on Albion fans that this might really be their season.

On Easter Saturday Albion brushed aside a poor Barnsley side – and their ex-Baggies management team of Steve Parkin and Tony Ford – 3-1, with Benjamin making a scoring start to what would be a brief Albion career. Bob kicked his heels in the dug-out – and never got the chance to renew his acquaintance with Kevin Miller — but his time, as it had two years before, was about to come.

On the Saturday, Wolves had won 3-0 at Burnley, but on Easter Monday their game at home to Manchester City kicked off early, as the two top teams met in front of the TV cameras. Before the game, Wolves manager Dave Jones was talking about catching the Mancunians, and winning the title; by the time Albion kicked off their game at Highfield Road, Wolves had gone down 2-0 and Albion needed a win to pull level on points. "At Coventry, on the bus from the hotel, we knew Wolves were getting beat. Then we were doing the warm-up, and the Albion fans were cheering, we knew something had happened, and when we went back into the dressing room before the kick-off, we were told it was 2-0. That gave us the incentive, but it also put the pressure on us. And we started off fantastic, putting the pressure on, and with a bit of luck I could maybe have had another two or three goals. The goal was another tap-in; in that short space of time, I must have had three vital tap-ins, from a yard – Forest, Coventry and Palace — which is unbelievable. I've never had a run where goals have come so easily, so simple."

Whilst Coventry never looked like scoring, Albion were just as incapable of getting the second goal to close the win. In the 62nd minute Megson took off Taylor and Dichio, and sent on Dobie and Benjamin, which led to a hectic finish when the Leicester man was sent off, but Albion held on for the win. "I enjoyed playing alongside Trevor. A cracking goal on his debut, against Barnsley – and then sent off on his away debut. I think he had a fulfilling month with us…"

On Friday April 5, Wolves lost at Millwall, giving Albion, for the first time, the chance to leapfrog over them – if they could get at least a point from their televised Sunday game against Rotherham. Prior to the game, Bob paid tribute to an Albion legend of the past who had helped him become the player he was. When Bob first joined the Albion, Ronnie Allen, who helped out with the coaching, was a huge influence. "He would tell me to strike through the ball, and to always have confidence if you miss. I never ignored what Ronnie had to say; everything he said made sense. And he was always there for me if I wanted to practise to improve my technique. Those lessons in the basics are still part of my game."

Early in the game against Rotherham, Bob broke a bone in his left hand, but he remained on the pitch to put Albion ahead in the 32nd minute. "I had to mark the keeper on a corner. I jumped with him, and I think my hand got caught in his loose jersey, and then he went one way and I went the other. I didn't really feel anything, but when I ran out, I was in agony, when my hand flopped around. I looked at it, and my finger was twisted double, and there was this huge lump. It was dislocated, and I put it back in, but I had to call Nick Worth over, and he taped it up. Ten minutes later, we were attacking, and Derek gave me the ball. I cut in, and put a shot low into the far corner. A good goal, good finish."

But the Rotherham game will not be remembered for Bob's goal; instead, it was a referee's decision which swung it. Darren Byfield equalised for the Millers, but Albion were robbed of victory because none of the officials saw that a shot from Jordao that had crossed the goal line, and was not given. The decision was doubly important; not only did it deprive Albion of a vital two points – at the end of the season, it spared Rotherham, and condemned Crewe to relegation instead. "That was the goal that never was. What can you put it down to? The linesman said he was obstructed down the line – but the player and the ball, when he cleared it, was in the net! It could have cost us, but it didn't. If it had cost us, there would be a lot of grief. But it didn't – it just made it more exciting at the end!"

That same evening, the Albion Supporters Club held its *Player of The Year* Night. Initially, the atmosphere was a little subdued because Albion had blown their chance to open up a three point lead over the Wolves – and Bob was a little late! "I had to have my hand X-rayed. Nick Worth and I went to the private hospital, and we had to wait nearly an hour and half, because there was nobody there! The X-ray department was shut, and the girl that ran it was at a barbecue! I think Nick was getting a bit frustrated about the wait, and was playing his face, but we got it done. I was phoning home, because I couldn't get back because I couldn't drive. So my wife had to bring my suit in, and I had to go to my mate's house to get changed, and we were ten minutes late getting to the do."

When he did finally arrive, Bob was surprised to find himself the inaugural winner of the *Jeff Astle Memorial Cup*. This was a trophy that had been donated in memory of 'The King' who had died in the previous January. Bob received a standing ovation and he was overcome with emotion as he collected his prize. "I think it means more because it's in the name of somebody who the fans adored and looked up to – a real legend at the club. And more so because his family had given the Astle Award on his behalf. I spoke to his wife and daughter, and they said that Jeff was often talking about me — that I could score goals, and I was a good player. That was a great honour, and a lovely award to have, but the best thing about it is that we can honour a great name from the past every year from now on. It's something special for the player, but it's great for the fans to celebrate Jeff's memory every year."

Albion's next game – at Bradford on Saturday April 13 – was now the most important of the season; Wolves were not playing until the Sunday, so the game was the perfect opportunity to open up a four point gap, and turn the screw on their rivals. Albion took over 6,000 fans to Valley Parade, a ground which had never been a happy hunting ground for them; almost certainly there was nobody present that day who had been there the last time Albion had won a League game on the ground seventy two years before.

"I was sub again. On the day, it looked as if it had got 0-0 written all over it. I'm not blowing my own trumpet, but in the last fifteen minutes, after I'd come on – fresh legs, and all that – that's when it all changed. I could have had two or three goals. The one when it came over the top of the defender was a bad miss, because I didn't place it wide enough. I should have just hit it as hard as I could. Then we got the penalty. It was a great ball from Dekka. Mooreo was going to head it, but I told him to leave it, and I chested it down. The lad who was marking Darren came to me, and I touched it forward. He committed himself, and if you get hit in the box, you're going to go down. But he did make contact, I know that for sure. He caught me just inside the knee. I wouldn't say it was bad, but you go down and it makes the referee's mind up as well. But I didn't want to take the penalty. Oh, no, no, no!"

As if in slow motion, referee Dean pointed to the spot. The crowd went crazy and grown men burst into tears, and it seemed an eternity before Bob had received his treatment from the Albion physio, and Igor Balis stepped up to take the most important penalty kick in the club's history. Although the penalty taker for the Slovakian national side, it was only his second one for the Albion – following that in the penalty shoot-out at Cambridge. No matter – in the fourth minute of added time, the full-back stroked the spot kick past Combe, and the game was won. Albion – and Bob – were just one win away from the Premiership!

"Igor had to have nerves of steel to take the penalty like that. When I was sitting on the floor getting treatment, I was looking round, and I could see the fear on the fans' faces. I didn't want to look. When Igor took the penalty I was on the side of the pitch and I looked at our fans rather than the goal. I just couldn't look. That was a good day, a fantastic day."

The next day was not so great, as Wolves beat Wimbledon 1-0 to leave them in third spot, a point behind the Baggies, setting up a week unique in Midlands football, one in which offices and factories across the Black Country were divided as never before, all arguing the chances of the two sides. On the final Sunday of the season, Albion would enter-tain Crystal Palace, who included an ex-Wolves striker who had always been a regular scorer against them, in Ade Akinbiyi. Wolves, mean-while, had to travel to Sheffield Wednesday – the club that Gary Meg-son once supported and played for.

In the build-up, the 'Golden Tit,' Sir Jack Hayward, said he had had a vision that Wolves would win at Hillsborough and Akinbiyi would score a hat-trick at The Hawthorns. Never have straws been clutched quite so desperately! The parallels with the game against Charlton two years before were obvious, although, as Albion kicked off in the bright sun-shine of another beautiful afternoon, the stakes were very different. Then, the club was desperately trying to avoid relegation to the Second. This time they were bidding for a place at the top table of English football.

Bob, his wrist bandaged after his fall against Rotherham, was making his 18th start of the season in the League. So many times had he been Albion's saviour – particularly with his goals in the 1993 promotion sea-son and against Charlton in 2000 – now he would score one of the goals that would take Albion to the 'Promised Land.' "I knew I was in the team two days before, when we did the set pieces; the gaffer said he wanted to go for experience, which was great for me. And when it was announced, Derek McInnes was telling me, 'This is written in the script for you. You couldn't write it any better. You're going to score the winning goal.'"

There was a surprise for all the players in the dressing room before the game. "The gaffer was telling us about all the times through the season that we'd been away from home, stopping in hotels and being away from our families. Then he nodded and said, 'This is who you've been doing it for' – and the door opened and in come these kiddies. And we thought 'What the hell's going on?' And that's when we started to see all the wives as well, all carrying these little Baggie Birds. 'Take a good look; this is who you're going out for today. These people, who you've put through hell to get here to day.' And it worked. The press would have had a field day if it had backfired. A bit of kidology, a bit of this, a bit of that; a masterstroke."

After two minutes Danny Grenville had a spectacular shot tipped over the bar by Russell Hoult. That was Palace's only chance of the game. In the 17th minute, man-mountain Darren Moore got on the end of a Neil Clement free kick to sidefoot Albion ahead. At Sheffield, Wolves had taken a first minute lead, but Wednesday equalised and, in the 53rd minute, went in front. A minute after that, at The Hawthorns, came Bob's moment of destiny. Hayden Mullins fouled Adam Chambers. Clement took the free kick – a poor one by his standards – but the ball bounced awkwardly in front of Kolinko. The goalkeeper allowed it to bounce off his chest and Taylor, following up as he had done at Forest and Coventry, stroked the ball home at the Birmingham Road End, just where he had scored against Charlton in May 2000.

"It was a bit wider than the Forest free kick, but I did exactly the same. I pushed into the ball, then spun off. Mullins, the lad who should have been marking me, didn't track back with me. I didn't know what the keeper was doing, but it did take a funny sort of bounce, as he went to try and catch it, and he spilled it, I just put it in. It was brilliant."

From then on it was an Albion party. Bob, his job done, left the field to a standing ovation in the 66th minute, although he desperately wanted to stay on to the end. At the final whistle, in scenes which mirrored another famous Albion game against Charlton – the one that clinched promotion to the top flight in 1931 – thousands of fans invaded the pitch.

When the pitch was eventually cleared, Bob returned, with his daughter Chantelle – it was her birthday – to soak up the atmosphere. He dedicated his goal to another great striker who had graced that same pitch. "I was delighted to win the *Jeff Astle Memorial Cup*, and this is a day to remember Jeff. My goal was for his memory." Albion were back in the top flight, where they belonged, and where Jeff Astle had played most of his games for the club.

Bob's dearest wish, recorded on TV that day, was to score a Premiership goal for the Baggies, but fortune so far has not been kind to him in 2002-03. Although he hardly played in Albion's pre-season programme (scoring at Tiverton Town and at Stevenage Borough) he did at least make it onto the bench for Albion's first-ever Premiership game, against Manchester United at Old Trafford. Albion lost the game 1-0 and Bob played the last seven minutes in place of Sean Gregan. At the start of the season Bob had had a hint from Megson that his three main strikers would be Roberts, Dobie and Dichio, so it was no surprise that he did not start against Arsenal or Leeds. For the fourth game of the season, Bob moved down another rung on the ladder, when Albion signed a new striker – Lee Hughes, the prodigal son, back from Coventry.

Albion won their first game in the Premier thanks to a goal from Darren Moore. Hughes had a promising start to his second spell at the club, running himself into the ground, to be replaced by Bob in the 78th minute. It was then that Bob came within a whisker of getting his longed-for goal, in the last minute of the game. Fulham, pushing strongly for an equaliser, had a corner, which was cleared straight to Bob, who was unmarked, just inside his own half. "The ball was played in over the top and the keeper came out and played it straight to me. I was in the

Bob's scored, and we're in the Premier!

136

centre circle, thinking I'd better keep hold of it, and visualizing the gaffer screaming and shouting at me if I'd lost it, like he does. But then I thought – no, might as well try it. And I connected sweetly, like a perfect golf shot, ideal height, with draw and everything. I honestly thought it was going in, and it would have done if the keeper hadn't been six foot six! But he just got there and tipped it over. Beckham? I think I would have retired there and then if it had gone in!"

Bob's first goal of the season proper came for the Reserves, against Birmingham City at The Hawthorns, when he raced onto a last minute clearance from Brian Jensen. A fortnight later Bob scored the Reserves' winner at home to his old club, Bolton. On September 30 Bob got his first start in the senior side, in the Monday evening game against Blackburn. Neither he nor the rest of the team played particularly well, as Rovers won 2-0. Then Bob bought a new pair of shoes! "It was a silly injury. I bought some new boots and they rubbed my Achilles tendon the wrong way, because of the way they were cut at the back, or something. So I've had to have two month's rest. The problem was, I kept playing and training instead of resting straight away, and I aggravated it. But now I've come back, and everybody's been given a chance except me."

Bob was sidelined until January 22, when he returned to the Reserve side for a goalless draw with Blues at Solihull Borough's Damson Lane ground, later going on to score a cracking headed equaliser against a very strong Everton line-up at Widnes RFC on March 12. "I've come back, I've had two weeks of hard running and physical fitness that you would normally do in pre-season. I'm fit, but you can't keep that fitness by training with the kids. I don't train with the first team, I train with the YTS. It's not like training and playing with first team players – you lose it that way. And it's a mental thing. You want to do things right, but it's never going to get you noticed."

And, as his Testimonial season draws to a conclusion, Bob remains waiting for the call to arms, hoping, once again, to play his part for his beloved West Bromwich Albion. In his ten years with the club, he had made a thrilling journey from the Third Division, right to the pinnacle of British football. "Getting to the Premiership is the greatest thing that I've done in my career, from a team point of view. This is what we all look to as players, fans and staff. But there are things which are even more important. Nobody can take away the adulation I've had from the fans, or the admiration I've had for them. It works both ways. It's something I've given, and it's something the fans have given, and it's something that no one man can take away from me. It's something I'll never, ever forget."

Bob's career appearances and goals for Leeds United, Bristol City, Albion and Bolton

Leeds Utd	L	LC	FA	FMC	PO
1985-86	2	-	-	-	-
1986-87	2	1+1(1)	-	1	1
1987-88	27+5(9)	4(2)	1	2(1)	-
1988-89	2+4	-	-	0+1	-
TOTALS	**33+9(9)**	**5+1(3)**	**1**	**3+1(1)**	**1**

Bristol City	L	LC	FA	AG	FMC
1988-89	12(8)	-	-	-	-
1989-90	37(27)	2(2)	7(5)	1	-
1990-91	34+5(11)	4	1	-	1
1991-92	13+5(4)	0+1	1+1	-	1(1)
TOTALS	**96+10(50)**	**6+1(2)**	**9+1(5)**	**1**	**2(1)**

Albion	L	LC	FA	AG	AI	PO	Fr
1991-92	19(8)	-	-	-	-	-	1(1)
1992-93	46(30)	2(1)	4(3)	4(3)	-	3	7(5)
1993-94	42(18)	4(1)	1	-	4+1(2)	-	6
1994-95	38+4(11)	1	0+1	-	-	-	7+1(5)
1995-96	39+3(17)	4(3)	1	-	5+2(3)	-	7(2)
1996-97	16+16(10)	2	0+1	-	-	-	8(3)
1997-98	11+4(2)	3(1)	-	-	-	-	4+1(2)
TOTALS	**211+27(96)**	**16(6)**	**6+2(3)**	**4(3)**	**9+3(5)**	**3**	**40+2(18)**

Bolton W.	L	LC	FA	PO
1997-98	10+2(3)	-	-	-
1998-99	32+6(15)	3+3(1)	1	3(2)
1999-00	15+12(3)	3+2(1)	3+1(2)	-
TOTALS	**57+20(21)**	**6+5(2)**	**4+1(2)**	**3(2)**

Albion	L	LC	FA	PO	Fr	
1999-00	8(5)	-	-	-	-	
2000-01	17+23(5)	2+1	0+1(1)	0+2	4+3(3)	
2001-02	18+16(7)	3	0+1	-	4+2(2)	
*2002-03	1+2	-	-	-	2+1(2)	
TOTALS	**44+41(17)**	**5+1**	**0+2(1)**	**0+2**	**10+6(7)**	

CAREER TOTALS

L	LC	FA	AG	AI	FMC	PO
441+107(193)	**38+8(13)**	**20+6(11)**	**5(3)**	**9+3(5)**	**3+1(1)**	**7+2(2)**

To date (March 16 2003), Bob has played in 523+137 first class games, and scored 228 goals for Albion, Leeds, Bristol City and Bolton Wanderers.

Albion Reserves

	CL	PLN	BSC
1991-92	-	-	-
1992-93	-	-	-
1993-94	1(1)	-	-
1994-95	1	-	1
1995-96	1	-	1
1996-97	7(3)	-	2(1)
1997-98	8(4)	-	-
1999-00	-	-	-
2000-01	6(2)	-	-
2001-02	4(1)	-	
*2002-03	-	9(3)	-
TOTALS	**28(11)**	**9(3)**	**4(1)**

Abbreviations: L: League, LC: League Cup, FA: FA Cup, AI: Anglo-Italian Cup, FMC: Full Members Cup/Zenith/Simod Cups, CL: Central League, BSC: Birmingham Senior Cup, PLN: Premier Reserve League (North), Fr: friendlies/Testimonials   *2002-03 figures as of March 17 2003

Bob's Favourite Goals

1. The diving header against the **Wolves**, at The Hawthorns, in 1995. Jimmy Greaves said it was a great goal, and you can't get a better recommendation than that!

2. The overhead kick, again at The Hawthorns, against **Bolton** in 2000. That was special because it was voted as the Albion's *Goal of The Season*, by the people who knew best – the Albion supporters themselves. Plus, it was against the club I'd just left, and had a couple of good years at, Bolton.

3. My debut goal against **Brentford**. At The Hawthorns – at the Brummie Road End – in 1992. You always want to do well in your first game for your new club.

4. The **Crystal Palace** goal last season; because of what it meant for the club, the players and the supporters.

5. My 'mazy dribble' at Kenilworth Road, against **Luton**, in 1994. I haven't dribbled like that since I was a baby…

6. The volley against **Bolton** at Burnden Park in 1992. It was slightly behind me, so I had to hit it a little on the turn. I like it because of the cleanness of the strike.

7. The header at St. Andrews, against Birmingham, in 1997. It had power, it was a last minute winner, it was against the **Blues**. What more could you ask for? I kissed my badge after scoring, and a Blues fan stopped me the following day, and said, "Our players don't do that; the passion's there, Bob!"

8. My Albion hat-trick goal, against **Watford**, in the 4-4 draw at The Hawthorns in 1996. Richard Sneekes played me in, and I slipped it past the keeper. That meant a lot after getting so many braces for the Albion, to get the hat-trick at last.

9. The header against **Plymouth** in the Coca Cola Cup at The Hawthorns in 1992. A good header – but it was special to score past Peter Shilton!

10. The shot that won the game against **Wycombe** in the FA Cup replay in 1992. I hit it sweet as a nut, but also because it got us out of a hole, because Wycombe should have beaten us that night.

Bob's Favourite Games

1. **Crystal Palace**, last season. For the importance, and the atmosphere, before and after the game.

2. **Swansea**, in the Play-offs, at The Hawthorns. If you weren't there, it's impossible to describe the atmosphere to you. You had to be there…

3. **Swansea**, at the Vetch Field, in the Play-offs in 1993. It was a poor game, but I will always remember it for Daryl's goal which was so vital, and gave us a chance.

4. My debut against **Brentford**. The pleasure of scoring that day, of all days, because the pressure was on me because I was replacing Don Goodman, who had been the fans' favourite. It was tremendous for me that the fans took to me so quickly.

5. Wembley, the Play-off Final against **Port Vale**. When you're a kid, it's one of your dreams that you want to play there, and that was my first 'proper' visit. Unforgettable.

6. **Sheffield United**, last season. There'll never be another game like that in the history of the Albion. Unique.

7. **Bradford** last season. Just for the last fifteen minutes, and the feeling when the final whistle went, and we'd won it. I'll never forget the crowd scenes that day.

8. **Portsmouth**, at Fratton Park, in 1994. The crowd scenes there were amazing, and that was the game which kept us in the First Division the year after we'd won promotion.

9. The 2-1 win at Molineux in 1994. My celebration may have failed after the goal, but the atmosphere that day made it the best **Wolves** Derby I've played in.

10. **Blues** away, in 1997. The new manager, Ray Harford, was watching from the stands. When fans talk to me now about Blues-Albion games, it's always the one when I knocked the two goals in. We really needed a win that night – and that time the team delivered.

11. For **Bolton**, when I came on as substitute, at The Hawthorns, in 1998. Even though it was only the last couple of minutes, I'll never forget the reception I got from the Baggies fans.

12. A match I never played in. The 3-2 win at home to the **Wolves** in 1993. I listened to it, itching in my boxer shorts in my front room; Darren Bradley's goal in that was fantastic.

THE BOB TAYLOR ALBION GOAL COLLECTION

Below we record, match by match, every goal that Bob scored for West Bromwich Albion, 1992-2002, including friendlies. The figure listed in parenthesis is the goal time. Games are League games unless otherwise stated.

1991-92

Albion 2 Brentford 0 (*Taylor, Fereday*) Feb 1 1992
1. (11) Put away on the right by Gary Robson, a debut goal with a shot under the keeper
Birmingham City 0 Albion 3 (*Taylor 2, G Robson*) Feb 8 1992
2. (26) A spectacular diving header after Fereday's shot had been saved
3. (71) A scoop over the line from Graham Harbey's cross
Bournemouth 2 Albion 1 (*Taylor*) Feb 22 1992
4. (90) Last minute toe poke home from a free kick
Bury 1 Albion 1 (*Taylor*) March 14 1992
5. (8) Superb overhead kick from out of the blue
Gibraltar 0 Albion 4 (*Taylor, Robson, Harbey, Cartwright*) Friendly March 17 1992
6. (30) A volley from a Craig Shakespeare cross
Albion 2 Bolton Wanderers 2 (*Taylor, Ampadu*) April 4 1992
7. (71) Bob nipped a cross off the feet of Winstanley to poke the

Goal 2: Bob's diving header, his first goal against Birmingham City

ball home

Albion 3 Preston NE 0 (*Taylor, Ampadu, West*) April 25 1992

8. (31) A header from two yards, from a West cross and Ampadu knock-back

Shrewsbury 1 Albion 3 (*Taylor, Strodder, Shakespeare*) May 2 1992

9.(37) Fine shot from a Gary Hackett cross; the last game under Bobby Gould

1992-93

Evesham Town 0 Albion 4 Fr (*Taylor, Robson, McNally, og*) July 18 1992

10. (26) 20 yarder which crept inside the near post to beat goalkeeper Taylor

Hereford United 0 Albion 1 Fr (*Taylor*) July 22 1992

11. (12) A blind side header from Simeon Hodson's free kick from the left

St Albans 0 Albion 7 Fr (*Taylor 2, McNally 2, Hackett, Ampadu, Robson*) July 25 1992

12. (31) Bob stroked the ball home after playing a one-two with McNally

13. (84) A diving header after Steve Lilwall had headed the ball on

Albion 2 Sheffield Wed 2 Fr (*Taylor, Ampadu*) July 30 1992

14. (43) A simple tap in from a good square pass from Kwame Ampadu

Goal 8: Bob converts Colin West's header, two yards out

Albion 3 Blackpool 1 (*Taylor 2, McNally*) Aug 15 1992
15. (20) A Fereday cross, and a deft Taylor header from twelve yards
16. (75) A superb volley to put away a loose clearance, from fifteen yards
Albion 1 Plymouth A 0 LC (*Taylor*) Aug 19 1992
17. (27) A fizzing header from McNally's free kick – past Peter Shilton!
Albion 2 Bournemouth 1 Aug 25 1992 (*Taylor, Shakespeare pen*)
18. (37) A header at the far post to a Lilwall cross, the first goal conceded by Bartram all season
Fulham 1 Albion 1 Sep 5 1992 (*Taylor*)
19. (2) 100 seconds into the game, Garner crossed superbly from the left and Taylor glided his header home
Albion 3 Reading 0 (*Taylor, Garner, Shakespeare*) Sep 9 1992
20. (87) Gary Robson set up Taylor from a close range left footer
Bolton Wanderers 0 Albion 2 (*Taylor 2*) Sep 15 1992
21. (55) A powerful header just inside the post from Coldicott's right wing cross
22. (83) Gary Hackett crossed for Bob to hook the ball home with a sensational overhead kick
Stoke City 4 Albion 3 (*Taylor 2, Garner*) Sep 19 1992
23. (25) Debut keeper Parkes miskicked a goal kick to Bob, who ran the ball home
24. (70) An equaliser with a stunning header from a Fereday cross

Goal 24: A stunning header in the 4-3 defeat at Stoke

Albion 2 Rotherham Utd 2 (*Taylor, Donovan*) Oct 24 1992
25. (37) A powerful header from a Coldicott cross, following a short corner

Albion 3 Hartlepool Utd 1 (*Taylor, Blissett, Robson*) Nov 3 1992
26. (6) Shakespeare curled in a free kick and Taylor headed across goal, and inside the far post

Albion 8 Aylesbury Utd 0 FAC (*Taylor, Donovan 3, Hamilton, Robson, McNally, Raven*) Nov 18 1992
27. (40) A looping header over the keeper, from a Lilwall cross from the left

Wycombe W 2 Albion 2 FAC (*Taylor, Bradley*) Dec 6 1992
28. (43) Ian Hamilton laid the ball on for Bob to shoot past Hyde from 18 yards

Albion 1 Wycombe W 0 FAC (*Taylor*) Dec 15 1992
29. (81) Taylor took down a Hamilton pass to shoot just inside the post

Albion 4 Walsall 0 AGT (*Taylor pen, Donovan, Hamilton, Heggs*) Jan 5 1993
30. (82) Methven fouled Taylor in the box, and Bob took the penalty himself

Albion 3 Bolton Wanderers 1 (*Taylor, Strodder, Hamilton*) Jan 9 1993
31. (71) A break out of defence finished off by Taylor

Mansfield Town 0 Albion 1 AGT (*Taylor*) Jan 12 1993
32. (49) Taylor and Sinfield both went to head the same ball, which

Goal 34: A great header at Bloomfield Road, from Hamilton's cross

looped over the keeper

Albion 1 Stoke City 2 (*Taylor*) Jan 23 1993

33. (16) Bob chested down a Bradley through ball and fired home a great shot

Blackpool 2 Albion 1 (*Taylor*) Feb 6 1993

34. (60) A classic headed equaliser from Hamilton's overhead flick-on

Albion 4 Fulham 0 (*Taylor pen, Hamilton, Mellon, Fereday*) Feb 13 1993

35. (2) Stannard fouled Speedie, and Bob put away the 100th goal of his career from the spot

Stoke City 2 Albion 1 AGT (*Taylor*) Feb 16 1993

36. (50) A scrambled goal, after inadvertently stopping a Hamilton shot

Stockport County 5 Albion 1 (*Taylor*) Feb 20 1993

37. (42) Speedie brought down a cross for Bob to smack it into the corner

Albion 2 Burnley 0 (*Taylor, Garner*) March 6 1993

38. (70) Bob ran onto a Burgess punt, dispossessed Davis and shot past Beresford

Brighton 3 Albion 1 (*Taylor pen*) March 10 1993

39. (47) A routine penalty kick, after the keeper had brought down Micky Mellon

Albion 3 Preston NE 2 (*Taylor 2, Mellon*) March 24 1993

Goal 39: SuperBob puts away his first League penalty, at Brighton

40. (7) Taylor diverted a powerful goalbound header past Farnsworth

41. (82) Ampadu headed a high ball down for Taylor to poke it over the line

Bradford City 2 Albion 2 (*Taylor pen, Hunt*) March 28 1993

42. (11) A penalty after a dubious dive in the area by Simon Garner

Albion 3 Swansea City 0 (*Taylor 2, Hunt*) Apr 7 1993

43. (2) A chip over the keeper after a good challenge by Hamilton

44. (16) A Mellon through ball, and Taylor lifted the ball over a defender to head past the keeper

Albion 2 Plymouth A 5 (*Taylor, Donovan*) Apr 12 1993

45. (9) Donovan and Hamilton inter-passed brilliantly to set up an easy goal

Mansfield Town 0 Albion 3 (*Taylor, Hunt, Heggs*) Apr 17

46. (26) Picked up a loose ball, beat two men and shot in from the edge of the box

Reading 1 Albion 1 (*Taylor*) Apr 21 1993

47. (35) A bullet header from a Hamilton cross, to put Albion in the Play-offs

Albion 5 Wigan Athletic 1 (*Taylor 2, Mellon, Donovan, Raven*) Apr 24 1993

48. (41) Taylor took advantage of a slip by Johnson to equalise

49. (88) A simple tap-in from a good, low Heggs' cross

Rotherham Utd 0 Albion 2 (*Taylor, Raven*) May 1 1993

50. (89) The ball forced over the lien from close range, from Heggs' cross

Goal 54: A header in the 4-1 home defeat by Palace

146

Albion 3 Hull City 1 (*Taylor, Hunt 2*) May 8 1993

51. (35) A Donovan cross which Taylor headed through the keeper's legs

1993-94

Albion 2 Southend United 2 (*Taylor 2*) Sep 1 1993

52. (52) A far post volley – Bob's first goal in 13 games

53. (57) Bob beat one defender, lifted the ball over another, for a superb goal

Albion 1 Crystal Palace 4 (*Taylor*) Sep 18 1993

54. (26) An unchallenged header from Hamilton's corner – Bob's 100th League goal of his career

Albion 1 Middlesbrough 1 (*Taylor*) Sep 25 1993

55. (48) A shot just inside the post, after some deft footwork by Paul Raven

Derby County 5 Albion 3 (*Taylor, Hunt 2*) Oct 3 1993

56. (53) A header after Hamilton had headed down at the far post

Chelsea 2 Albion 1 LC (*Taylor*) Oct 6 1993

57. (44) A forty yard run that ended with a shot past Kharine from 18 yards

Albion 1 Pescara 2 AIC (*Taylor*) Oct 12 1993

58. (45) A diving header from a Gary Strodder head down

Albion 3 Peterborough Utd 0 (*Taylor 2, Strodder*) Oct 16 1993

59. (47) Bob climbed to beat two defenders and head in a Hunt cross

60. (59) An unchallenged header to a cross from Neil Parsley

Albion 4 Watford 1 (*Taylor, Hunt 2, Hamilton*) Oct 30 1993

61. (51) A swivel to put away Donovan' cross

Goal 59: The opening goal at home to Peterborough United

Albion 2 Bolton Wanderers 2 (Taylor pen, Hunt) Nov 6 1993
62. (44) A comfortable penalty past Russell Hoult after Davison
had been sent off for wresting Bob to the ground
Albion 4 Portsmouth 1 (*Taylor, Hunt 2, O'Regan*) Nov 27 1993
63. (17) A lay-off from Hamilton slid home by Bob
Southend United 0 Albion 3 (*Taylor, Hunt, Hamilton*) Dec 11
1993
64. (66) Slipped under the advancing keeper after Hunt had missed
Ashcroft's cross
Cosenza 2 Albion 1 AIC (*Taylor*) Dec 22 1993
65. (17) A half volley to put away a loose ball on the edge of the
box
Grimsby Town 2 Albion 2 (*Taylor, Fenton*) Feb 1 1994
66. (81) A scrambled equaliser after Mardon's shot had been
blocked
Wolverhampton Wanderers 1 Albion 2 (*Taylor, Mardon*) Feb 26 1994
67. (32) A McNally tackle led to the ball squirting out to Bob, who
placed it past Stowell
Albion 3 Notts County 0 (*Taylor 2, Hunt*) March 16 1994
68. (45) A volley from a loose ball ten yards out, following a corner
69. (63) A great header from an Andy Hunt cross
Oxford United 1 Albion 1 (*Taylor*) April 12 1994
70. (24) A far post shot from a Hamilton free kick that was headed
on by Donovan

Goal 71: A late consolation goal at the City Ground

Nottingham Forest 2 Albion 1 (*Taylor*) April 23 1994

71. (82) A great shot into the far corner, after stumbling

Luton Town 3 Albion 2 (*Taylor, Ashcroft*) May 3 1994

72. (55) The best goal ever? A sixty yard run that ended with a poke under the keeper

1994-95

Swansea City 0 Albion 3 Fr (*Taylor 2, Donovan*) Aug 2 1994

73. (3) A perfect header from a McNally cross

74. (30) Bob chested down a Mike Phelan cross and flicked it past the keeper

Cardiff City 2 Albion 3 Fr (*Taylor 2, Donovan*) Aug 6 1994

75. (88) A header from a perfect Donovan cross

76. (90) An unlikely last minute winner, on the deck, from a Mellon pass

Luton Town 1 Albion 1 (*Taylor*) Aug 13 1994

77. (4) Bob raced onto an Edwards pass to fire home from twelve yards

Millwall 2 Albion 2 (*Taylor 2*) Sep 10 1994

78. (10) Nipping in to take McCarthy's poor back pass, Bob rounds Keller to score

79. (55) A header from eight yards after Jeroen Boere flicked on Ashcroft's long throw

Albion 1 Burnley 0 (*Taylor*) Sep 24 1994

80. (71) A glancing near post header from Ashcroft's free kick

Goal 81: A gift of a goal, for a change, at Stoke's Victoria Ground

Stoke City 4 Albion 1 (*Taylor*) Oct 2 1994

81. (31) Muggleton dropped Lilwall's cross at Taylor's feet, for a tap in

Charlton Ath 1 Albion 1 (*Taylor*) Nov 13 1994

82. (55) A sweet volley to a great cross from Carl Heggs

Albion 3 Oldham Ath 1 (*Taylor, Ashcroft, Donovan*) Nov 19 1994

83. (85) A close ranger header from an Ashcroft cross

Albion 4 Gothenberg 1 Fr (*Taylor, Donovan 2, Raven*) Jan 29 1995

84. (58) A sidefooted finish from six yards from Smith's cross

Portsmouth 1 Albion 2 (*Taylor 2*) March 8 1995

85. (43) A speculative shot from 25 yards that goes straight through keeper Alan Knight

86. (88) A vital winner. volleying home after a great run by Paul Agnew

Albion 2 Wolverhampton Wanderers 0 (*Taylor, Ashcroft*) March 15 1995

87. (48) SuperBob is back – a classic diving header from Ashcroft's perfect cross

Albion 5 Tranmere Rovers 1 (*Taylor, Ashcroft 3, Donovan*) Apr 30 1995

88. (84) A shot inside the box from Ian Hamilton's pass

Goal 94: A cool finish in the 2-1 win at Boundary Park

1995-96

Albion 1 Aston Villa 0 Fr (*Taylor*) Aug 1 1995
89. (67) A chip from the right, flighted beautifully over Bosnich
Albion 1 Northampton Town 1 LC (*Taylor*) Aug 15 1995
90. (41) A glancing header from a Tony Brien cross
Wolverhampton Wanderers 1 Albion 1 (*Taylor*) Aug 20 1995
91. (46) A perfect header after Hunt had beaten Shirtcliff to cross from the left
Northampton Town 2 Albion 4 (*Taylor 2, Hunt, Donovan*) Aug 22 1995
92. (45) Sent away by Hunt, Bob shot home from eight yards
93. (72) A close range shot. after Woodman had saved his first effort
Oldham Ath 1 Albion 2 (*Taylor, Gilbert*) Sep 9 1995
94. (11) Mardon's free kick was helped on by Hunt, for Taylor to coolly slot home
Albion 1 Huddersfield Town 2 (*Taylor*) Sep 30 1995
95. (36) Put away after a great through ball by Andy Hunt
Albion 2 Reading 0 (*Taylor, Gilbert*) Oct 7 1995
96. (65) Donovan intercepted a Bernal pass and crossed for Bob to sweep the ball home
Albion 2 Reggiana 1 AIC (*Taylor, Hunt*) Nov 8 1995
97. (75) A far post shot from Andy Hunt's cross
Brescia 0 Albion 1 (*Taylor*) AIC Dec 13 1995
98. (87) A roll in on the snow from Ian Hamilton's through ball, to earn a semi-final tie

Goal 96: Bob sweeps home a pass from Kevin Donovan, against Reading

Ipswich Town 2 Albion 1 (*Taylor*) Feb 3 1996

99. (66) Bob's first League goal for four months, blasting a Hunt pass into the top corner

Albion 3 Southend Utd 1 (*Taylor 2, Hunt*) Feb 10 1996

100. (46) Bob bundled home after Gilbert's shot had been saved

101. (86) Slid home from a Paul Holmes cross

Albion 1 Oldham Ath 0 (*Taylor*) Feb 27 1996

102. (37) A shot from ten yards after Hunt had hit the post

Albion 1 Port Vale (*Taylor*) March 2 1996

103. (18) Smith beat Porter and crossed for Bob to slam home from close range

Port Vale 2 Albion 1 AIC (*Taylor*) March 5 1996

104. (72) A far post header from an Ashcroft corner that seemed to have earned a place at Wembley

Albion 4 Watford 4 (*Taylor 3, Sneekes*) March 12 1996

105. (13) A low drive from a Donovan pass

106. (27) A precise shot from Shane Nicholson's pass

107. (79) Cut inside from a Sneekes pass, to score his first Albion hat-trick – at last!

Watford 1 Albion 1 (*Taylor*) March 23 1996

108. (78) Bob swept home a fine pass from Julian Darby

Albion 3 Grimsby Town 1 (*Taylor 2, Sneekes*) Apr 13 1996

109. (25) A well placed header from Sneekes' cross

110. (29) Slotted home from inside the box after a well-worked move involving Butler and Sneekes

Goal 119: It's always good to score against the Wolves...

Norwich City 2 Albion 2 (*Taylor, Sneekes*) Apr 20 1996
111. (30) Swept into the net from Andy Hunt's low cross
Albion 3 Derby County 2 (*Taylor, Sneekes, Hunt*) May 5 1996
112. (89) An offside tap-in after Hunt's shot had been blocked, to beat the champions
Albion 3 Coventry City 2 Test (*Taylor, Gilbert, Donovan*) May 6 1996
113. (28) Scored from a Holmes cross at the second attempt

1996-97

Albion 2 Port Vale 0 IOM (*Taylor, Hunt*) July 24 1996
114. (80) A rebound from a Peschisolido shot
Albion 1 Bury 0 IOM (*Taylor*) July 27 1996
115. (41) A chip over Bracey after the keeper had kicked a goal kick straight to Bob, to win the Isle of Man Cup
Hereford United 2 Albion 2 Fr (*Taylor, Raven*) Aug 3 1996
116. (63) The Hereford keeper drops the ball at Bob's feet – another twelve incher!
Charlton Ath 1 Albion 1 (*Taylor*) Aug 24 1996
117. (10) A poke over the keeper after a scramble in the area
QPR 0 Albion 2 (*Taylor, Peschisolido*) Sep 7 1996
118. (87) A far post push over the line from David Smith's mis-hit shot
Albion 2 Wolverhampton Wanderers 4 (*Taylor, Hamilton*) Sep 15 1996
119. (66) A good finish after being sent away by Shane Nicholson

Goal 126: Bob celebrates the winner at Bramall Lane

Albion 1 Port Vale 1 (*Taylor*) Nov 9 1996
120. (36) Two yards out – after Musselwhite had been jolted by his own defender, and dropped the ball
Albion 2 Bolton Wanderers 2 (*Taylor pen, Peschisolido*) Dec 8 1996
121. (80) Bob sent Branagan the wrong way from the penalty spot, to earn a point
Albion 3 Oxford United 3 (*Taylor, Sneekes, Hunt*) Dec 21 1996
122. (90) Another late point-saver, from a yard, after Hamilton had hit the post
Albion 1 Oldham Ath 1 (*Taylor*) Jan 18 1997
123. (45) A great overhead kick from Gilbert's corner and Nicholson's flick-on. The last Albion goal under Alan Buckley
Birmingham City 2 Albion 3 (*Taylor 2, Sneekes*) Feb 4 1997
124. (32) A magnificent header from Hamilton's corner
125. (90) A great late winner, a header at the far post from a high Hunt cross
Sheffield United 1 Albion 2 (*Taylor, Coldicott*) Apr 5 1997
126. (71) A hook shot, on the turn, from Dave Smith's pass

1997-98

Halesowen 0 Albion 6 Fr (*Taylor 2, Hunt, Kilbane, Hughes, Peschisolido*) July 19 1997
127. (10) Forced a mis-hit shot from Andy McDermott over the line
128 (41) Slid a hard low Andy Hunt cross over the line
Luton Town 1 Albion 1 (*Taylor*) LC Sept 16 1997
129. (35) A header from a teasing Smith cross

Goal 130: Bob scores his first goal in almost a year at Oxford

Oxford United 2 Albion 1 (*Taylor*) Feb 17 1998
130. (63) Headed home a Hughes cross, for his first League goal in almost a year
Albion 2 Port Vale 2 (*Taylor, Flynn*) March 21 1998
131. (83) A bullet header from a great cross from Sean Flynn; the last goal of his first spell at the Albion

1999-00

Barnsley 2 Albion 2 (*Taylor, Sneekes*) Apr 8 2000
132. (56) A brilliant looping header from van Blerk's free kick – the first goal 'back home.'
Albion 4 Bolton Wanderers 4 (*Taylor, Sneekes pen, Flynn, Oliver*) Apr 15 2000
133. (79) A acrobatic overhead kick ten yards out
Albion 2 Grimsby Town 1 (*Taylor 2*) Apr 24 2000
134. (15) A diving header from Sneekes' free kick
135. (48) A scrambled goal from close range, following a free kick
Albion 2 Charlton Ath 0 (*Taylor, Sneekes*) May 7 2000
136. (70) A great Clement cross, a looping header over Kiely, to ensure Albion's safety

2000-01

Greve 0 Albion 4 Fr (*Taylor, van Blerk, Richards, Hughes*) July 20 2000
137. (8) Quinn's cross headed home powerfully from eight yards

Goal 144: A classy finish — Bob lobs the Tranmere keeper in a 2-1 win

Notts Co 0 Albion 3 Fr (*Taylor 2, Quinn*) July 28 2000
138. (25) Brave diving header at the near post from an Adam Oliver cross
139. (68) Gentle header to a precise chip from Des Lyttle
Albion 1 Birmingham City 1 (*Taylor*) Sep 17 2000
140. (2) Took a van Blerk pass, beat two defenders and lashed the ball home from ten yards
Derby County 3 Albion 2 FAC (*Taylor, Hughes*) Jan 6 2001
141. (76) Good header from a Jason Roberts cross
Albion 2 Crewe 2 (*Taylor, Roberts*) Feb 20 2001
142. (23) First time shot swept home from a Ruel Fox cross
Albion 2 Tranmere Rovers 1 (*Taylor 2*) March 25 2001
143. (39) A lay-off from Sneekes, for Bob to lash home just inside the post
144. (62) Picked up on a defensive error to lob the keeper – a class goal
Burnley 1 Albion 1 (*Taylor*) April 14 2001
145. (83) A vital late headed equaliser from Ruel Fox's cross

2001-02

Greve 0 Albion 6 Fr (*Taylor, Hughes, Clement, Dobie, A Chambers, Quinn pen*) July 17 2001
146. (87) A crisp finish to Adam Chambers' back header
Slagelse 1 Albion 3 Fr (*Taylor, Fox, Roberts pen*) July 19 2001

Goal 136: Bob heads the vital deciding goal against Charlton

147. (35) A close-range (offside!) poke home from Lee Hughes' flick-on
Stockport County 1 Albion 2 (*Taylor 2*) Oct 16 2001
148. (9) A fine left-footed volley from fifteen yards
149. (60) Bob put away the rebound after the keeper had saved Neil Clement's far post header
Crystal Palace 0 Albion 1 (*Taylor*) Oct 31 2001
150. (63) A neat pirouette past two defenders, and toe-poke home from close range
Nottingham Forest 0 Albion 1 (*Taylor*) March 22 2002
151. (82) A crucial diving header from twelve inches after Clement's free kick had hit the bar
Coventry City 0 Albion 1 (*Taylor*) Apr 1 2002
152. (16) A striker's goal – from a foot out – after Jordao had missed a sitter
Albion 1 Rotherham Utd 1 (*Taylor*) Apr 7 2002
153. (32) Bob's best of the season, a shot across the keeper from the edge of the area
Albion 2 Crystal Palace 0 (*Taylor, Moore*) April 21 2002
154. (54) The predatory goal that put Albion into the Premiership – Bob slots home from close range after a dreadful error by Kolinko

2002-03

Tiverton Town 0 Albion 2 Fr (*McInnes, Taylor*) July 25 2002
155. (79) Scott Dobie's low cross was scooped home by Bob from inside the six yard box.
Stevenage Borough 0 Albion 4 Fr (*Johnson, Dichio, Taylor, Clement*) August 10 2002
156. (81) A superbly taken half volley from Balis' cross

Goal 150: Bob is ecstatic after scoring the only goal at Palace

FRIENDS OF
BOB TAYLOR

001	Lesley Taylor	057	June Northall	113	Nathan Reynolds
002	Chantelle Taylor	058	Mick Northall	114	Charlie Reynolds
003	Calum Taylor	059	Ian Hoult	115	Martin Foster
004	Donald Taylor	060	Derek Tudor	116	Jason Southall
005	Glenda Taylor	061	Mike Kinson	117	Trevor Southall
006	John Homer	062	Laura Kinson	118	Keith Weston
007	Dave Holloway	063	Steve Matthews	119	Julie Stevens
008	Vicki Ashfield	064	Jeff Prestridge	120	Ernie Williams
009	Sarah Jane Homer	065	Dave Prestridge	121	Chris Penn
010	David Homer	066	Jeff Hassell	122	David Penn
011	Kevin Grice	067	David Mills	123	Julie Walton
012	Valerie Willmore	068	Dean Walton	124	Bob The Wulf
013	Joan Willmore	069	Syvia Nock	125	Ben Chance
014	Dorothy Ingram	070	Jean Banks	126	Robert Hinsley
015	Daniel Grice	071	Malcolm Banks	127	Mark Clapham
016	Amanda Hume	072	Joan Beynon	128	Keith Robinson
017	Lynn Challis	073	A W Turner	129	Matt Ferguson
018	Edith Brownhill	074	Andrew Rogers	130	Christine Wilkinson
019	Arron Brownhill	075	Rachael Fletcher	131	Dick Peck
020	Trevor Challoner	076	Nick Fletcher	132	Janet Cotterill
021	Barry Raybould	077	Dougie Webb	133	Alan Cotterill
022	Adrian Mark Hill	078	S A Moss	134	Rob Hewlitt
023	Adam M. Whitehouse	079	Adrian Dudley-Evans	135	Duncan Cameron
024	Craig A.Whitehouse	080	Philip Shaw	136	Alistair Partridge
025	Mark A. Whitehouse	081	John A Castle	137	Tony Wilcox
026	Karen Wright	082	Robert S Bradley	138	Fitz Robinson
027	Barry McNeill	083	Barry Brisland	139	Paul Ellis
028	Steve Cannon	084	Audrey Cooper	140	Mike Phipps
029	James Bell	085	Ian Tubby	141	Shell Phipps
030	Dale Baxendale	086	Pete Sargent	142	Stuart Clarke
031	Peter Baxendale	087	Chris Purdon	143	Craig Clarke
032	Robert Aiken	088	Olive Bullock	144	David Russell
033	N G Walker	089	Martin Bullock	145	Alan Cleverley
034	Allan Timmins	090	Julian Rowe	146	Peter J Gregory
035	Steve Waterhouse	091	Keith Wibberley	147	Tony Snape
036	Richard Jones	092	Andy Croydon	148	Shaun Hipkiss
037	Garry John Wheeler	093	Simon Wall	149	George Prest
038	Mel Turner	094	Peter Wall	150	Jonathan Clive Round
039	Martin Dawes	095	Chris Marsh	151	Jonathan Want
040	Paul Collins	096	Adam Pressdee	152	Mark Swallow
041	Dave Walker	097	Amanda Palfrey	153	Gail Swallow
042	Lisa Hicks	098	Steve Hale	154	Laura Swallow
043	Geoffrey Whitehouse	099	Richard Barton	155	Jack Swallow
044	Andrew Whitehouse	100	Oliver Willmore	156	Sarah Swallow
045	Clive Blake	101	Mick Bryan	157	Ben Moss
046	Graham Belt	102	Andy Price	158	Ian Price
047	Alan G Wheatley	103	Matthew Price	159	Michael Gough
048	Mark Bell	104	Justin Price	160	Tim Green
049	Dave Fryer	105	Bob Price	161	Darren Knight
050	Andy Heselgrove	106	Stephen Walsh	162	Darren Tranter
051	Callum Heselgrove	107	R Priest	163	Steve Morris
052	Darren Cooper	108	Mark Skellon	164	Sophie Morris
053	Chris Cadman	109	Phil Surridge	165	Ellie Morris
054	Paul Ellis	110	Paul Harrison	166	Paula Beardsmore
055	Andy Wilce	111	Richard Powers	167	Taylor Poole
056	Thomas Northall	112	Neil Reynolds	168	Phil Foster

169	Elliott Bromley	232	Claire Hughes	295	Stephen James Blandford
170	Ciaran Bromley	233	Jenny Hughes	296	Sarah Moseley
171	Gaynor Brookes	234	David Warner	297	Janet Bennett
172	Mark Brookes	235	Christine Marks	298	Jamie Arowsmith
173	Aaron Luxton	236	Colin Mackenzie	299	Trevor Westwood
174	Lew Clews	237	Dave Knight	300	Alan W Deane
175	Jonathan Russel	238	Gavin Johnson	301	Sheila M Deane
176	Steven Hadley	239	Cavan Timmins	302	Paula Ellis
177	Raymond Hadley	240	Tom Grice	303	Lee Ellis
178	Nicolas Hadley	241	John Rowe	304	Andrew Brough
179	Brian Androlia	242	Paul Ward	305	Elizabeth Goodby
180	John Hickman	243	Roger Fallon	306	David Carpenter
181	Shaun Blackwell	244	Judith Hunt	307	Paul Carpenter
182	Peter Lyons	245	Rachael Hatfield	308	Richard Oakley
183	Paul Homer	246	Michelle Bennett	309	Dave Dolton
184	Chris Flanagan	247	Stuart Bennett	310	Darren Whitehead
185	Tim Radford	248	Dave Bunt	311	Stefanie Wood
186	Clive Smith	249	Darren Somers	312	Sarah Clarke
187	Ami Batham	250	A J Timmins	313	Stephen Carr
188	Emily Batham	251	Michael Thomas	314	Jamie Greensill
189	Alan Brettell	252	Gavin Paul	315	Dave Bowater
190	E N Perrins	253	Louise Collieu	316	Simon Branson
191	Paul Roberts	254	Gary Peniket	317	Matthew Dunn
192	B P Walters	255	Stephen Cloves	318	Mike Vass
193	Adam Cooper	256	Derek Linney	319	Esther Wellman
194	Peter Hall	257	James Linney	320	Christopher Moore
195	Taylor Ellis	258	John Walker	321	David Moore
196	Mick Corfield	259	Malcolm Calder	322	Keith Melhuish
197	**Wally Henvey RIP**	260	Sharon Cartwright	323	Lucy Farnell
198	Tony Lloyd	261	Peter Turner	324	Jemma Farnell
199	Roy Martin	262	Peter Turner	325	Jeff Burges
200	Andy Lawford	263	Leroy Wright	326	Chris Hall
201	Cathy Maddox	264	Richard Mountford	327	B Walker
202	John Maddox	265	Charles Waldock	328	Bob Moulah
203	Michelle Price	266	Jack Cheshire Eden	329	Roy Cooper
204	Darren Price	267	Roy Hayden	330	L Barnsley
205	Bryan Grundy	268	Veronica Williams	331	J M Barnsley
206	Kate Reece	269	Keith Williams	332	Jonathan Eden
207	Philip Houghton	270	Iain Graham	333	Verity Eden
208	Kristy Nicholls	271	Alan Graham	334	John Aldridge
209	Ryan Parton	272	British Heart Foundation	335	Michelle Lyons
210	Stephen Hyde	273	Gerard Small	336	Darren Lyons
211	Dale Summers	274	Michael Joyce	337	Daniel Collins
212	Dave Taylor	275	Kim Biggs	338	Arthur Grady
213	Cole Payne	276	Carl Scott	339	James Meighan
214	Alistair Dengate	277	Jenny Wheale	340	Steve Gregory
215	Jean Zoeller	278	John A Holmes	341	K Pegler
216	Jenny Harrison	279	Rhys Suban	342	Andy Taylor
217	Chris Dawson	280	Ian Sedgley	343	Timothy Duggan
218	Mark Pearsall	281	Andy Grove	344	Steve Savkovic
219	Archie Ryan	282	Simon Payne	345	Gloria Hunter
220	Jim Sherwood	283	Roberto Marrocco	346	Trish Conford
221	Beth Horton	284	Thomas Grigg	347	R L Birks
222	Barry Venables	285	Carol Haynes	348	Howard Jennings
223	John Pietralski+family	286	Claire Hunt	349	Bob Jeavons
224	Darren Crump	287	Carl Bradford	350	Stewart Evans
225	Steve (Badger) Hinks	288	Dave Siviter	351	Adam Darby
226	Michael Field	289	Abbie Jane Mansell	352	Luke Turner
227	Jim Price	290	Gary Lockley	353	Darrin Shepherd
228	Neil Price	291	Norman Baxter	354	Neil Bell
229	Kev Martin	292	Margaret Neale	355	C D Vine
230	Helen Martin	293	David Valder	356	Michael Baxter
231	Jack Martin	294	Michael Cartwright	357	Geoff Lawday

Bob's 1993 Promotion side

Stuart Naylor. A good shot-stopper, hard to beat... and loved a drink!

Tony Lange. A big frame, good reflexes; a lump of a bloke, who did really well in the Play-off games.

Nicky Reid. Mr. Fitness, a great athlete, a perpetual motion man who fully deserved his Final *Man of The Match* Award.

Steve Lilwall. What can I say? Came from non-League football, won his place and kept it. A great character in the dressing room – always 'himself.'

Darren Bradley. A good captain – one of the lads, down to earth, a genuine guy.

Gary Strodder. A tough, non-nonsense character, who did a great job. No frills – but no fear either, and rock solid in the Final.

Paul Raven. A good footballer, an honest lad who had a good understanding with both Burgess and Strodds.

Daryl Burgess. A 100% performer, very solid, who scored the vital goal at Swansea, but who was so unlucky to miss the Final.

Kevin Donovan. A fantastic player, with great skill, and a joy to play with. He was a striker's dream, creating lots of chances with great intelligence and movement.

Bernard McNally. A genuine player whose enthusiasm could lift the side – and a great player on the ball.

Ian Hamilton. A 'cockney' lad — who loved his clothes! An underrated team player, who was a good laugh, and he didn't let criticism affect him.

Gary Robson. It was sad that he didn't get on at Wembley. Loves the Albion, and looked after me when I joined. Always got stuck in!

Andy Hunt. Best striking partner I ever had. A strange lad! We hit it off straight away, and he was always good for a goal.

Simon Garner. An experienced player, and I learned a lot from him in a short time. he helped to steady the younger lads, and Wembley rounded off his season.

Bob's 2002 Promotion side

Russell Hoult. He should play for England. Best goalie I've played with, always one to make the vital save.

Larus Sigurdsson. No-nonsense defender and hard man, who takes no prisoners!

Darren Moore. His very presence won us games in 2001-02. A brave player who plays through injury, as solid as a mountain, and proud to be an Albion man.

Phil Gilchrist. His Premiership experience is invaluable; he understood what was needed to get us out of Division One. A lot of injuries didn't stop him.

Igor Balis. Mr Cool. Given a chance; and he took it. Good pace. His penalty at Bradford assured his place in Albion folk lore (Has anybody named their baby Igor yet?)

Neil Clement. Loads of potential. A quiet lad who takes things to heart. A great left foot – and some great goals.

Andy Johnson. A bargain buy. Runs all day, box to box, and takes a lot of pressure off the back three.

Derek McInnes. A good captain, who looks after everyone. he got us organised and drove us on. Came back from injury and proved he could last the pace. A great inspiration to us all.

Adam Chambers. Young and full of running. Did a job and deserved his glory (and got the free kick against Palace!)

Michael Appleton. A terrible blow when he was injured. Until then he was player of the season. Always running, and a terrific tackler.

Scott Dobie. A big culture shock for him, but he did great. His early season goals kept us going, and he learned a lot, quickly.

Daniel Dichio. A big lad who scored vital goals. Took the burden up front, added a new dimension to our play, and did a good job defensively.

Jason Roberts. A class act. Unlucky during the season. Came back when Scott's goals dried up – then missed the rest, when the goals were spread around the side.

Des Lyttle. Straight up and down, supporting the attack. Never let the side down – and my golf partner!

Jordao. A good passer of the ball, with some vital strikes – at Wolves for instance! A cultured player with silky skills.